By the Editor

Start off Smashed!
In Search of Eastern Promise
Victory in 'Site'!
If It Wasn't for Golf . . . !
By Yon Bonnie Links!

DURBAN'S LADY IN WHITE

An Autobiography

Perla Siedle Gibson

Compiled, Edited and Introduced
by Sam Morley

Aedificamus Press

First Published 1991
Aedificamus Press, The Ridgeway,
Northaw, Herts, EN6 4BG
All rights reserved. No part of this book
may be reproduced or transmitted
in any form or by any means, without
permission from the publishers.

© 1991 Joy Liddiard

Typeset by Ryburn Typesetting Ltd, Luddendenfoot, Halifax

Printed in Great Britain by
The Amadeus Press Ltd, Huddersfield

British Library Cataloguing in Publication Data
Gibson, Perla Siedle
 Durban's Lady in White: an autobiography.
 1. South Africa. Social life, 1939–1948 – Biographies
 I. Title   II. Morley, Sam
 968.055092

 ISBN   0-9511701-3-9

Contents

List of Illustrations

Introduction
by Sam Morley

Perla Siedle Gibson opens her autobiography with:

'"Hey! Ma-a-a. . .", they shouted, they yelled, they cried. I cried, too.

It was April, 1940. I was standing at a Durban dockside canteen, being called "Ma" by thousands of young khaki-clad soldiers lining the rails of the a giant troopship slowly gliding by.

"Sing us a song, Ma!", "Come on, be a sport, Ma!", "Give us Land of Hope and Glory, Ma!". . .

I cupped my hands wide over my mouth. At the first notes of that most moving of patriotic songs a hush fell. Then a full-throated chorus of thousands took up the refrain. . .

Thus started my wartime career, for which Destiny had prepared me over the previous thirty years via the concert platforms of the World.

Over the ensuing five years I sang to well over 1,000 troopships and 350 hospital ships. . .'

Invitations to write an Introduction to this story were politely refused when one or two big names were approached – on the grounds that those days were enshrouded in the mists of time and getting thoughts and feelings into focus now would be impossible.

Then came an off-beat idea. The Lady in White had cast

her spell over millions of ex-Service personnel, the vast majority of whom had 'sat below the salt', so to speak. So why not stop searching among the top brass and Burke's *Peerage*, and persuade one of that vast majority to tackle it. Like the ex-leading seaman on the the other end of this pen. After all, Destiny might well have selected him, too, for the job over fifty years ago! Look at the evidence:

1.   When volunteering for the Navy in 1940, I was found to be slightly red/green colour blind and about to be rejected. But Destiny intervened. The examiner took pity on my misery and had me go through the patterns again, dropping a helpful word or two second time round. (*Had to promise, though, that when watch-keeping on a ship entering or leaving harbour, I'd call for a second opinion on red and green buoy lights when approaching the entrance, in time to avoid crunching an expensive warship into the wall!*).

2.   After nearly two years on east coast convoys with a 34-year-old V & W destroyer, HMS *Verdun*, I joined HMS *Redoubt* being built in John Brown's yard, Glasgow. We left Scotland with the rest of our flotilla in November, 1942, – escorting a large convoy bound for the Cape and on to Mombasa, then the main base of our Far Eastern Fleet. But Destiny intervened. *Redoubt* was detached from the convoy for a chain of unpredictable and unconnected duties that had us – with our sister ship, *Racehorse*, – rushing around the Mediterranean, back to Scotland, across the Atlantic to Norfolk, Virginia, down to Curacoa in the West Indies, back to Gibraltar, down to Casablanca and down the African coast with another big convoy. Whereby it wasn't until April 1943 that we reached Durban. Just in time to be told by the Admiralty that instead of joining up at last with our flotilla and the Fleet at Mombasa, Destiny had decided that we be seconded to a newly-formed South African Navy

HMS Verdun 1940 to 1942.

HMS Redoubt 1942 to 1944.

The two 'floating hotels' on which I spent a total of four years *en route* to 'Destiny'. (Ed.)

HMS Dorsetshire: 8 8''-gun County-class Cruiser whose torpedoes finished off the *Bismarck* off Brest in May 1941. One year later the Lady-in-White sang to survivors of *Dorsetshire* and her sister ship *HMS Cornwall* when brought into Durban by hospital ship after both were sunk by Japanese dive-bombers off Colombo. (Perla's story, page 109.)

patrol-and-escort force that had us operating around the Atlantic and Indian Oceans for the ensuing eight or nine months. During which time we often steamed in and out of Durban Harbour, where sight and sound of the Lady became a familiar part of the scene.

3.   In 1988 I wrote a light-hearted book in which one chapter tells of a 1987 South African tour with a party of friends. Destiny had me describing our arrival at Durban as follows:

'Coaches waited to take us to the 38-storey Maharani Hotel on the Durban ocean front, and all rooms looked down on to the same surf-pounded beaches on which I was almost swept out to sea 45 years earlier, when *Redoubt* had lain alongside Maydon Wharf between convoys, and I was diving through the breakers on a few hours' shore leave.

Maydon Wharf should have nostalgic memories for hundreds of thousands of British and Allied forces, I wrote, whose troopships would pile into Durban harbour for provisions and fuel before proceeding up to the battle zones of Egypt and Burma. When entering or leaving those safe waters, a lady dressed in white flowing robes would be standing at the end of the jetty and in a rich soprano voice would sing 'Land of Hope and Glory', 'Now is the Hour', 'Will ye no come back again', 'Bonnie Mary of Argyll' and dozens of other familiar songs to the fascinated troops lining the crowded decks, as the ships steamed slowly through the narrow entrance. I must have experienced this half a dozen times or more, but it was always a moving occasion – and in fact still is as I write about it.

Although I don't remember actually witnessing the scene close up – probably because on a 'pusser' ship one needed to be smartly clad in whites to appear on the upper deck when entering or leaving harbour, and I preferred to stay in a pair of grotty shorts while fiddling with the ship's electrics between decks. The lady's voice, however, would be clearly heard from below and the singer often glimpsed from a crowded lobby entrance as we passed – thereby providing a dramatic close-up in the mind's eye.'

4. For the past four or five years a young lady in our village has done my secretarial work – between catering for the needs of a large house, her husband John, three children, and two ginger cats. Helen Wightwick, née de Beer, was born, bred and schooled in Cape Town. When converting my scribble into legible typescript for the book in question and working on the paragraphs quoted, she phoned from home to say that my famous but unknown-to-me Lady was the aunt of her best friend at school (*that same best friend, Barbara Siedle, has since proved a great help in my research for the final pages of this book.*) The flowing white robes to which my manuscripts referred, said Helen, never existed. Any time an Allied warship, troopship, hospital ship or supply ship entered or left harbour, Perla Siedle Gibson (for that was my unknown Lady's name) who did voluntary work in the forces canteen near the harbour entrance, would come out and go through the singing routine – still wearing her white canteen overall-coat! [*So much for that 45-year-old dramatic close-up in the mind's eye!*]

Now with a world population of about three billion, only Destiny could have so shuffled the cards to have had Helen de Beer come to England some seventeen years earlier, get married, settle down in a village not two miles from my home, and take on part-time secretarial duties for me whereby her knowledge in this matter was to be of such significance.

5.   I seldom watch TV or listen to the radio at home, and since retiring from business in 1982 it isn't often I'm on the commuter-laden highways between 5.00 and 7.00pm – which is when John Dunn hosts a music-and-chat show on Radio Two every weekday and has been doing so for umpteen years. I don't suppose I hear any part of it more than a couple of times a year. Yet on 19th January 1990, Destiny had me homeward bound from a rare afternoon meeting in town. The Paverotti cassette my daughter had given me for Christmas had just ended with a dramatic crescendo, so I switched to Radio Two. Just in time to hear John Dunn say,

> "Countless people over the years have written or phoned to ask if I can shed some light on the mysterious Lady in White that sang to the ships at Durban during the 1939–45 War. Our team of researchers have tried without success. That is, until now. For they have found that although the Lady in question has long passed on, her daughter, Joy Liddiard, married an Englishman after the war and now lives in Sherborne, Dorset."

He introduced her and, among many things, she said that her mother had written an autobiography, published in South Africa in 1964, but that the publishers had made no effort to distribute the book abroad – despite pleas from her mother that she had so many friends in Britain, United States, Canada, Australia etc. who would want to read it. It had long since gone out of print and disappeared from South African shops. There were just one or two precious copies in national libraries and museums, and among some of the family members. She read us a paragraph or two.

Agog with excitement, I reached home and telephoned Directory Enquiries for the number of Joy Liddiard in Dorset. Destiny ensured that they had no trouble finding it and that the lady was at home when I rang. Complimenting her on how well she came over in the interview – how wound up I was while listening to it – how I'd not long written and published a book in which her mother had been featured and a copy of which would go in the post to her next day – I asked if it were possible to see her mother's book. So many would want to read it, no doubt, but in my case it would not only be personal interest in the story but the possibility of bringing out an English edition after all these years. Within three days the postman delivered one of her three remaining copies.

It was a beautiful but harrowing story that I took to bed that night. Reading with misted eyes into the small hours, I marvelled at this international concert star, pianist and painter, who – without faltering – dedicated five years of her life in using her talents to boost the morale of serving personnel being transported into horrific war conditions thousands of miles from their loved ones. As is said on the jacket flap:

'From April 1940 to VJ Day August 1945, in the early dawn, in wind, in rain, in the blazing sub-tropical sun, she never missed one convoy. Not even the one that sailed out the day she learned her eldest son had been killed in action while serving with the Black Watch in Italy.'

Many names of those who paid her homage and to which she proudly refers in these pages would be unknown to most of us today. But others, like Lord Louis Mountbatten, George VI and his Queen Elizabeth; Queen Elizabeth II and the Duke of Edinburgh; George Bernard Shaw; Noël Coward and top Allied officers were unsparing in their praise.

In the years after the War she was asked repeatedly to re-unions and remembrance services in all parts of the world. Here's her account of the 'hush-hush' appearance at a special BBC El Alamein programme on Trafalgar Day, 1955, hosted by Wilfred Pickles, after a similar attempt the previous year was aborted when London newspapers ferreted out the proposed surprise. This time she reached London Airport in secrecy and the BBC spirited her away from there 'under wraps'. Rehearsing with a full orchestra was a long tedious business but nothing leaked out this time. She writes:

> Came the great moment and, trembling with nervousness I waited for my cue. The television theatre was in total darkness. I could hear the soft, mellifluous voice of Wilfred Pickles sketching, in words, the scene at Durban docks in wartime, of my standing there awaiting the arrival of a convoy. . . . Then, from the violinist, crouching beside me in the darkness came the ping that gave me my note and cue. I burst into 'Land of Hope and Glory' as the theatre was flooded with light and stood there – in my white dress and my red hat, the megaphone raised to my lips – an exact replica of those dockside scenes of nearly a generation before. The secrecy this time had been fool-proof and the audience in the theatre, composed, at the special request of the War Office, of ex-soldiers who had passed through Durban, stared in momentary silent disbelief at this sudden materialization of memories they all shared, and then rose to their feet and cheered and cheered.
>
> It was a thrilling, moving experience. For the millions of viewers the picture they saw in their screens, I was told later, was a remarkably detailed

and accurate representation of Durban docks with, as it appeared, my walking up and singing directly at them just as if they were troops on board a ship.

Wilfrid Pickles was delighted. He told me he had never before achieved such an effect. 'You had them all in tears', he kept saying. 'But it must be wonderful for you to know that you brought happiness tonight into more than 8,000,000 homes.'

Dramatic details of a similar performance in 1964 with the Burma Star Association at the Royal Albert Hall is told in the same chapter, as is one with a Scottish flavour at Perth with the 51st Highland Division. Not to mention the visits she describes to the hospitals and homes for blind, limbless and other disabled veterans.

Joan of Arc created a legend in the 15th century when, at the age of 15, she donned her armour plus a visored steel helmet and, with sword in hand, inspired courage in her troops. Perla Siedle Gibson created one 500 years later, when, at the age of 50, she donned her canteen-coat plus a waterproof red hat and, with megaphone in hand, did something similar to ours. Maybe not in quite so vigorous a fashion, but equally stirring and effective.

Joan's epic story is often told by others in the world's history books. Here, for the first time, Perla tells her own to the world.

Thanks, Destiny, for choosing me to present it.

January 1991

The Lady-in-White on the cat-walk at the Crystal Palace TV station for the 'Ask Pickles' programme.

THE "LADY IN WHITE" IS BACK IN SCOTLAND

Her Voice Thrilled Three Million Soldiers

TODAY is the day the "Lady in White" arrives in Scotland — news to bring a thrill to thousands of Scottish soldiers whose troopships called at Durban during the war.

In fact, the "Lady in White" has three million boy friends.

Scots soldiers are very dear to her heart and especially The Black Watch.

Her son, Roy, a Black Watch lieutenant, received fatal wounds on a night mountain "recce" in the Italian campaign near Cassino.

Madame Perla Siedle Gibson, operatic singer and concert pianist, also has intimate associations with Dundee, although she has visited the city only once.

Major's Invitation

She has come from her home, Pineholme, Durban, South Africa, to spend a holiday with her married daughter, Joy, in Manchester. She has also accepted an invitation to stay a fortnight with Major Simon Crawford and his wife at their home Tigh-na-Chuillin, Lochearnhead.

The Major was one of the Scottish soldiers who became a life-long friend of the "Lady in White" when he met her at Durban in 1942.

She may not be able to visit Dundee during her present visit to Scotland, but she's arranged to rendezvous at Crieff with a Dundee friend.

Pen Friendship

Mrs Gibson and Mr Henry Cook, now of Pitlochry, will have much to talk about. Mr Cook, as a journalist, took part in a telephone interview from Dundee to Durban with Mrs Gibson to tell the first complete story of the lady who was meeting every troopship and singing to the men on their way to North Africa and Italy.

When Mrs Gibson visited Scotland in 1949, Mr Cook and his colleagues entertained her at a dinner.

A pen-friendship has continued ever since.

Mrs Gibson is 75. As a girl she prepared bandages for the wounded in the Boer War, and she first sang to the troops passing through Durban in the 1914-18 war.

Her father was a well-known Durban shipping man, and she was aboard a tug towing a ship out of harbour when the captain said, "Give them a song, Perla, as a parting gift."

"He handed me the ship's megaphone," said Mrs Gibson, "I sang the verses of popular songs of the day. The troops hung over the sides and sang the choruses, until they were cast off.

"Later, the ship's captain wrote to say how deeply the men had felt about it all."

Perla sang to many ships during that war.

She married in 1917.

In the years of peace, she trained in Berlin for opera.

She has sung with many of the famous concert conductors and entertained them at her home.

"When war broke out again and troopships began to call in at Durban, my mother was asked to take on the task of giving the troops refreshments.

"I was one of her many helpers on the quayside, and I was expected to sing. When a troopship entered the harbour I sang 'Land of Hope and Glory.' If it was a warship I sang 'Rule Britannia.'

"When the troops disembarked I sang whatever they requested, from grand opera to the very latest from Tin Pan Alley.

250 A Day

"But usually it was homely songs like 'Loch Lomond,' 'Jeannie With the Light Brown Hair' or 'I'll Walk Beside You.'

"Once I took a note of the number of songs I sang in one day, it totalled 250.

"Officers and men living all over the world write to me continually."

Her sons, Roy and Barry, joined the South African forces in 1939. They were sergeants in The 1st Transvaal Scottish Regiment, affiliated to The Black Watch RHR.

They were in the North African campaigns.

Her husband, Jack, who had been an officer in the 1914-18 war, was determined to be with them. He became a sergeant in the No. 2 Blood Bank Squadron of the S. African Air Force.

Roy was commissioned to the 6th Battalion Black Watch. He was killed in action on the heights of Mount Ornito, near Cassino, in 1944.

Prayer For Courage

He now lies in The Black Watch cemetery at Mintero. Barry and his father returned safely.

A fortnight after Roy died, Mrs Gibson's mother died.

"I am a great believer in prayer," she says, "and I prayed for courage. I know that as a result of that prayer I was able to go out to the dockside again and sing as I have never sung before."

She has sung more than 500 troopships in and out of Durban.

Security made ship movements a secret, but Mrs Gibson was regarded as "essential" and given entry to the movements' room.

She had a public citation in Natal, when it was said, "The 'Lady in White' is a household word wherever British troops are stationed."

With King and Queen

When George VI and Queen Elizabeth visited Durban in 1949, they asked Mrs Gibson to come and sit with them.

"I shall always remember the Queen's words — 'We thank you for what you did for the morale of the troops in the war.'"

She has been to Britain twice before. Requests for visits come to her from all over.

"But it is quite impossible to fulfil all of them," she says.

From *Dundee Evening Telegraph* August 15 1963.

Foreword
by Joy Liddiard

This book is brim-full of wonderful human stories and I welcome the opportunity to make the autobiography of The Lady in White available to the many who remember those wartime experiences; or in this new generation, have listened to stories told by parents and grandparents.

It has been difficult for me to read the book as it is packed with so much that I lived through with my mother. There is also much that I remember which has had to be left out – either for lack of space, or moments too personal.

Perla Siedle Gibson was my mother, whom I adored. She was so full of love for her family and for everybody she came into contact with. I am as amazed today as I was all those years ago at the miraculous fortitude and inner strength that enabled her to live through the physical and mental traumas she experienced. She was the perfect example of what she often told us as children – "the more you put into life, the more you will get out of it."

Even today the impact of her singing a welcome and farewell to those thousands of servicemen and women is still as strong and even more nostalgic as it was, and the press continue to receive and publish letters asking for information about the Lady in White. This publication of her autobiography is the result of the enquiries received before and after John Dunn interviewed me for BBC 2 on the 19th January 1990. The original book, now out of print, was published in South Africa in 1964 but never distributed in the UK – apart from the few copies brought over by my mother before her death on the 6th March, 1971 and given to friends. There must be many who remember those days, or who have heard of them, when troopships and their escorts put into harbour in Durban. After many weeks of dodging submarines, mines and torpedoes, to arrive in Durban to hear the voice of a loving motherly figure singing songs from home must have been balm to their hearts.

After the John Dunn broadcast, Sam Morley phoned me about the book. I was able to let him read my precious copy, after which, he wrote: "Her memory lives on, but there are very few who will have known the Perla Siedle Gibson as identified with her autobiography. I'd deem it an honour to be entrusted with re-publishing that book".

Indeed we are indebted to Sam for this and I do thank him most sincerely, on behalf of the many, whose hearts will beat a little faster "down memory lane". It is 27 years since the story of The Lady in White was first told and it is 20 years since she died, and still the letters come – her memory lives on, indeed.

Joy Liddiard

January 1991

Clockwise from top left: 1, Troopship getting the full treatment; 2, With nursing staff aboard Hospital Ship *Amra*; 3, With Mark 1 megaphone and hat; 4, A dockside close-up; 5, Aboard *Amra* with Mark 2 megaphone; 6, *HMS Nigeria* putting to sea after presentation of Mark 3, and final, megaphone; 7, Her precious dockside pass. (All explained and enlarged upon in the text).

Dedicated to the Great-Hearted who place service before self and in memory of those who made the Supreme Sacrifice.

Preface

by Perla Siedle Gibson

Like so many autobiographies this one owes its existence to the urgings of many friends the world over. They brought strong arguments to bear. There were so many, they said, who would rejoice in the memories that my story would revive. There were many others who would see in this book a reminder of loved one who failed to return; and there was a new generation since the war who would want to know more of my unique dockside career. And so I set to work, poring over masses of documents, recalling countless incidents and remembering the many people who contributed to making my life such an adventurous one.

When last visiting Britain, I received constant reminders that those who had passed through Durban in wartime had not forgotten the woman in white who had sung to them from the dockside. The warmth of the reception wherever I went and hospitality of the great and famous convinced me that my friends were right. 'The Lady in White' should tell her story. Here it is. The names of many organizations and people intersperse its pages, yet I am conscious of many omitted – not for any other reason but the limitations of keeping a story strictly within the bounds of readability.

I received encouragement and help from all sides and among the many letters was one from Lord Louis Mountbatten, who graciously permitted me to quote an extract:

'I am most interested to hear of your autobiography and am convinced that "The Lady in White" will be a great success – it will bring back the happiness you brought to so many servicemen in those dark years.

'I need hardly say that I have read the remarkable list of ships to which you sang, with astonishment and admiration.

'I should like to take the opportunity of wishing you the very best of luck with your autobiography which I know will be most interesting to read.'

(*Signed*) Mountbatten of Burma

I am most grateful to Merlin Morgan for his constructive interest and painstaking co-operation in the research that was necessary, and to Eve and Conrad Norton whose literary help made this book possible.

Durban
1964

— 1 —

My meeting with destiny

Hey! Maaaaa. . . . They shouted, they yelled, they cried. I cried, too. I had never been called 'Ma' in my life before and here I was, standing at a Durban dockside canteen, being called 'Ma' by thousands of young khaki-clad soldiers lining the rails of a giant black and grey troopship.

'Sing us a song, Ma.' 'Come on, be a sport, Ma.' 'Give us 'Land of Hope and Glory', Ma.'

The cries were taken up until the very air seemed to reverberate. To sing here in the open; on a stretch of quayside that was echoing to the roar of the giant cranes as they swung, endlessly, loads of war material into the holds of the waiting ships; where the tramp of marching feet as thousands of soldiers climbed the gangways kept up a staccato drumming, and where the morning air was punctuated by the mournful hooting of tugs, the shrill piercing whistles of trains and by the chugging of shunting engines – it was unthinkable. I had a mental picture of the look of horror such a prospect would have brought to the face of my London singing professor. I thought of the scores of occasions I had stood in the centre of a stage, a full orchestra poised below me, waiting for the final murmurings of the audience to die away before lifting my voice in song. And now, here I was being called upon to sing amid all the clamour and noise of a quayside that resembled at that moment some gigantic beehive in which activity never ceased for a moment.

Yet, I felt an inner compulsion. This was, I sensed, my

rendezvous with destiny. It was for this moment – and for the countless more like them that were to follow in the years ahead – that I had prepared myself, unknowingly perhaps in the accepted sense of the word, yet somehow subconsciously aware throughout my life that I would one day be called upon to do a duty for which God had equipped me.

Would my voice last a day – an hour – under such conditions? What did it matter! All that was important was that these men, leaving behind them all that they held dear, wanted one final, sentimental, reminder of home before their ships sailed, taking them to the battlefields from which so many were never to return.

I cupped my hands wide over my mouth. As the first notes of 'Land of Hope and Glory' rippled in the morning air a hush fell. The shouting voices were stilled, and, as I sang on, a full-throated choir of thousands took up the refrain until the entire harbour seemed to vibrate to the strains of that most moving of all patriotic songs. I sang on and on – all the lilting songs of World War I – 'Pack Up Your Troubles'; 'Will Ye No Come Back Again'; 'Its a Long Long Way to Tipperary', and, singing, I realized the moving significance of having been called 'Ma'. I vowed inwardly that come what may in the uncertain days that lay ahead, I would never fail those separated from their own loved ones who saw in me, standing alone, the yearning personification of all that home meant to them.

I was not to fail them because, I truly believe, Providence watched over me to see that I did not. I sang to well over 1,000 troopships and to more than 350 hospital ships, and never once did my voice or strength falter – not even when racked by personal tragedy.

This, then, was the start of a wartime career – the strangest and most rewarding that could possibly fall to me, a woman who had nothing more to offer to the cause for which men and women were dying in their thousands than a God-given voice and a burning determination to fulfil a destiny that had opened up before me, almost like a revelation, as I heard those dockside shouts for 'Ma'.

Physically, it must be conceded, I fitted the appellation. I was of medium build and somewhat on the plump side. I was 50 and married and the mother of three grown-up children. *Time* magazine was later to describe me as 'A smiling, stocky, Wagnerian soprano', and if, as I am sure it did, it conjured up in the minds of some who read it a somewhat formidable image, this was charmingly dispelled by the distinguished writer, Noel Langley.

> 'Such a description of her', he wrote, 'tends to create the impression that she goes about with a paste helmet clapped over one eye and a bent spear at the ready, intoning '"O-hee-you".'
>
> 'She did not,' he added, and then went on to say, 'She is the simplest, kindest heart I know. Most of us try our best to do the least possible damage to our fellow human beings. Without trying at all she has done either good – or nothing. I recall her standing there like a plump little everyday saint out of a Rubens freize, keeping her spirits flying through all weathers every time a ship of war hove to. She still trusts life; she trusts people; the Divinity which protects babies and drunks takes a little time off to protect her too.'

A generation has passed since the days I began singing at the docks, but the memories remain as vivid as if it all happened yesterday. In winter, the docks, cold and dreary, with a high wind lifting the spray from the crest of the waves and dashing it over the quay wall. And in summer the ships shimmering in the heat of the tropical sun as they lay in their drab, steel grey colours, waiting for the signal that would send them and their human cargoes to the far corners of the earth where freedom was fighting its grim battle for survival.

Whether it was four o'clock on a cold, blustery winter's morning; midday beneath the blazing sun, or that twilight hour when a gentle fading light softened the harsh contours of the troopships as they sailed out of harbour to the open sea, I was at my place on the quayside dressed in the 'uniform' that was to make me known as 'The Lady in White' – ousting eventually, somewhat to my regret, the familiar, homespun 'Ma'. How often I have thought of the strange twist of fate that was to make my fulfilment as an artist – to which I had devoted a lifetime of study and practice – materialize not on the conventional concert hall or the opera stage, but on that grime-encrusted stretch of quay. I have known the thrill of listening to the applause of rapturous audiences; of receiving the plaudits of the rich and famous. My memories are enriched by many moments of high drama that fall to those with artistic talent, but all that dissolves into nothingness compared with the richness of the rewards that were to be mine as a dockside singer.

There can be – and I say this in all humility – few singers in history who, in their lifetime, have achieved so universal a fame as was to be my privilege. Literally thousands of articles have been written about 'The Lady in White' in newspapers and journals throughout the world. I have, so I am told, been described affectionately in more servicemen's magazines than any other individual in World War II and believe that I am the only civilian woman in naval history to whom the ensign was dipped in salute by so many ships as they passed. Many honours have been bestowed upon me. King George VI, in 1946, graciously awarded me a Certificate of

Commendation, and from the citizens of my home town – Durban – I received the highest honour that the civic authorities are empowered to bestow. But these, too, fall into nothingness alongside the simple, heartfelt letters of thanks that I have received in their thousands from men and women round the world, and which today – more than twenty years later – I am still receiving. Frequently written in painstakingly correct phrases, and bearing postmarks of obscure towns and villages around the world, these letters tell of the happiness – the fleeting moment of happiness – that 'The Lady in White' was able to give them while their troopships lay in Durban harbour. Others are brief, poignant messages, telling of the death in battle of someone whom I only knew as one among thousands of anonymous figures in battle dress leaning over a ship's rails, and still others are words of thanks from naval captains for the moral uplift my singing gave to sailors weary and heartworn after weeks at sea.

Every artist recalls with pride the occasions when audiences reacted with warmth and enthusiasm; in their memories are enscribed, in exact detail, the places where they received this or that ovation. My thoughts, too, are filled with memories like these, only in my case there was but one place to which my audiences came from all over the world.

Durban, in wartime, was one of the major cross-roads of the seas. For hundreds of thousands of troops it was the first land they saw after as many as forty days at sea, and, after a brief stay, it was their point of departure for any one of half-a-dozen different battle areas. So Durban took on a very special significance in the minds of men, living under the constant strain of war, with all its easily conjured-up terrors. They were to recall it as their last point of contact with the sane, civilised life they once knew and into their memories were burned incidents that normally would have been nothing more than passing thoughts.

Thus it is that I know from letters received and from what I was told that merchant seaman stamping their feet to keep warm while standing watch in U-boat alley in the Atlantic would allow their thoughts to wander back to Durban and to wonder aloud if 'The Lady in White' still sang to the ships and when they would hear her again – if ever; that Desert Rats crouched in their slit-trenches in the Western Desert would hum nostalgically the songs they had last heard echoing across the ever-widening stretch of water between their ship and the Durban dockside; that the boys of the RAF on a Burma airstrip, the sun beating down on them, and men in the foetid jungles, would trace their thoughts back to Durban and to the singer standing there; that tough Australians would tell their cobbers of the woman who sang 'Waltzing Matilda', and that men of the Royal Navy, in submarines below the sea and in ships above, would yarn about the woman who wore a big red hat and sang all their favourite songs.

Could any artist, anywhere, at any time, have received so rich, so enduring, a reward for the simple task of singing songs? I think not. That is why I believe I was ordained by Providence to fulfil this particular wartime task and that I was given the strength and the power to carry it out without ever having to let down the troops, who, as the years wore on, came to expect, almost as their right, that I'd be standing there to sing to them. When I sang, I had a feeling that I was, in some way, like a pipe conveying life-giving water from a reservoir to a parched garden – the 'water' in this case being love and courage, and drawn from a source which I instinctively knew would never fail me.

Standing on a concert platform I would be almost a nervous wreck waiting for the conductor to bring down his baton, but never once felt this way with ships' audiences. There was, it seemed, almost a tangible link through which flowed the strength that enabled me to sing to them for hours on end. I sang hundreds of songs from hymns to the the latest jazz numbers. I often sang until I had what seemed a permanent crick in my neck through looking up at the ships and I would carry on singing until the very last moment just in case someone might be straining to catch the very last linking note with home.

What were my own feelings as I sang to those departing troopships? I hated most that moment when the hawsers were finally cast off and fell into the water with the dull plop of inevitability. There was no escaping the thought that among those on board there were many who were never to come back, but I would think of the song 'We'll meet again, don't know where, don't know when; but I know we'll meet again some sunny day'.

There have been many occasions since the war when 'We'll meet again' has come true for me, but none so dramatic as that which occurred only a few years ago. I answered the door and found waiting a short, pale-faced man, wearing thick-lensed spectacles. He looked at me and to my surprise said, 'You are just as I thought you would look – a sweet, motherly woman'.

His name was E.G. ('Bunny') Austin and he had been a regular soldier in the British Army. This was the story he unfolded. His parents, trapeze artists in a circus, had both been killed when they fell from the high wire. The young orphan ran away, but was found by the police and eventually put into the army on what was known as 'boy' service. He had had no schooling and couldn't read or write. When he was paid he 'signed' the receipt by means of a thumb-print, which soon led to his being nicknamed 'Thummie' by the other soldiers.

'So that the others wouldn't rag me I bought myself a reading primer and tried to teach myself to read. I'd study at night under the blankets by light of a candle, but one night I was caught and put on charge for "reading after lights out". Knowing my inability to read the Colonel refused to accept the charge, but on hearing my story he took me under his wing and I was sent to school. There I displayed an aptitude for music and I ended up in the regimental band.'

With the outbreak of war the regiment was drafted overseas. 'Bunny' Austin, on embarkation leave in London, found that his eyes were troubling him, but fearful of being taken off the draft and separated from his friends, he kept the fact secret. In Burma, fighting against the Japanese, his eyes grew steadily worse, until complete blindness set in and, as the war ended, he was shipped home to England in the Netherlands hospital ship, *Orange*. The ship stopped at Durban and the blacked-out world in which 'Bunny' was living was one day pierced by the sound of a woman singing. 'Bunny' recognized the voice of 'The Lady in White' – who had sung to his ship when it called at Durban *en route* for the East.

'You won't remember me, but I asked the nurse if you could come and speak to me because I remembered you so well. You came and spoke to me and after we talked you sang six songs. I've never forgotten how kind you were. I returned to England where they operated on me and – by a miracle – my eyesight was restored. I told my wife that one day I would go back to South Africa to thank you.'

And that was what he did. He signed up as a member of the ship's band on the *Dunnottar Castle* for a round-trip voyage from Southampton to South Africa. In my autograph book he wrote the words: 'I was blind. Now I see the picture I expected to see. How beautiful. Thank God.'

There are, in these pages, other accounts of how my 'We'll meet again' philosophy proved correct, but none, I think, as moving as that of 'Bunny' Austin.

And so, what is written in these pages is, for me, more than a mere recital of memories. The incidents that are recalled, the names that are mentioned evoke a deep sense of gratitude and humility that destiny should have bestowed upon me the privilege of carrying out a wartime task that brightened, to some small degree, the lives of those who had such dark and terrifying paths to tread in the cause of freedom. What is written here is, as I have said, a testament of my faith, and, if, as a book, it succeeds in reawakening memories among those who, more than a generation ago, heard me singing on the dockside, if it brings comfort to those whose sons and husbands failed to return, then it will have achieved its purpose and I shall have been doubly rewarded.

I believe that there is no such thing as an 'accident.' What happens in our lives is ordained and falls into a carefully planned sequence.

In the case of 'The Lady in White', it all dates back to 16 April, 1940, when my mother, an active social worker and chairwoman of the Women's Auxiliary of the Seamen's Institute in Durban, received an urgent telephone call from Defence Headquarters. She was asked if she and her helpers could provide refreshments, from our newly completed canteen on Maydon Wharf, for 800 Rhodesian troops arriving at Durban that day to sail for East Africa in the troopship *Karanja*. They were the first troops from southern Africa to leave for service abroad. There was a mad flurry to prepare the 800 boxes of sandwiches, cigarettes, sweets and clothing, but we managed it somehow. Looking back to that day, 800 seemed an astronomical number, but before the war ended our little canteen was to supply millions of such gifts and to serve, as well, meals to the embarking troops.

I, like the rest of the voluntary workers, wore what was almost a regulation uniform – a plain white dress and a white apron. It was as we bustled about doing the multifarious duties of attending to the troops as they started to embark that there came the shouts of 'Ma'.

The moment that was to change my life had happened.

—— 2 ——

The years of preparation

It was fitting that Durban should provide the backdrop, and the docks my improvised stage, for my family's roots are deeply embedded in the history of the city and inseparably linked with its bustling harbour.

My father, Otto, born in Woolwich in 1856, came from a Swiss family which for generations carried on the craft of watchmaking and bell-founding in the Black Forest before migrating to England, there to continue the family business. Love of music was a deeply ingrained family characteristic and two of my father's sisters, both opera singers of note, were invited to sing at the glittering opening of the Albert Hall in London in 1872.

In 1882 my father emigrated to Durban to become a book-keeper in the the shipping firm of King and Sons, the South African branch of the British shipping company, Bullard, King and Co., London. In those days a ship drawing more than six feet of water was not able to enter Durban harbour and my father had to be brought ashore from the outer anchorage by launch . . . a far cry, indeed when I think of the mighty ships which today glide through Durban's harbour entrance. Soon caught up in the warm hospitality of the then small Durban community, my father became the close friend of the Watson family, in which there were five daughters and a son. One of the daughters, Amelia Mary, was to become my mother.

The Watson family had been living in Durban since 1851 – they arrived by sailing vessel from England – and established a transport business in the then tiny settlement –

a mere cluster of houses in the area where today Albert Park slopes down to the bay. Two ox-wagons constituted the transport.

The fever that swept the country following the discovery of gold in the Transvaal set in train a vast movement of people determined to cash in on the 'El Dorado' then being uncovered. The Watson family decided to move to Ladysmith, then the railhead and the stepping-off place for all those bound for the goldfields of the Witwatersrand, and it was here that Otto Siedle married his Amelia in 1887. A year later, in Durban, in a neat bungalow set in an acre of garden, with lovely flowering indigenous trees, I was born.

The restive Watson family had, in the meantime, made another move, this time to the Witwatersrand, an arduous journey by ox-wagon that took several months. As a small girl I never tired of listening to the stories of the adventures which befell them. Two incidents, in particular, stand out in my memory, and they both concern snakes. Trotting ahead of the wagon that was drawn by eighteen oxen, Grandmother Watson suddenly saw a snake slither out of the long grass to attack. Terrified, she ran, but the faster she moved the faster the snake followed her until the wagon driver caught up with her and discovered that the snake's fangs were fixed in her tweed skirt. On another occasion a python swallowed a bush buck near a house in which Grandmother Watson was living and continued to thrust its small head through the wire netting of a fowl-run to swallow a fowl. The frenzied clucking of hens brought Grandmother Watson running to find the python lashing wildly in an effort to extricate itself from the netting in which it was firmly wedged by the two undigested bulges.

The goldfields failed to live up to the expectations of Grandfather Watson, and eventually the whole family returned to Natal, first to Ladysmith, and later to Durban.

They set up house in Currie Road, in what today is the Berea, and as his five daughters married, Grandfather Watson built each of them a house on the property that he had bought. All six houses were set in large gardens with an interlinking pathway. Our house was No. 15, and for seventeen happy years my four brothers and I lived here surrounded by the other members of the family, in what was generally known as the Watson Girls' Colony. The 'Big House', Lynneville, in which Grandfather and Grandmother Watson lived, fell to my mother as an inheritance and it was from that lovely home, redolent with family history, that I was married in 1917.

While still a small girl, it emerged that I had inherited something of the family's musical talents, and it was decided that I undergo training as a pianist in what was then – in 1907 – the world's musical capital, Berlin. My teacher was to be Herr Professor Martin Krause, a pupil of the great Liszt – assuming that was, that I measured up to the exacting standards that he expected of his pupils. With my mother I travelled to Berlin and on the great day I sat down, trembling, at the piano, while the Professor, in soft-soled shoes, paced to and fro, his hands folded behind his back in a way, when I think back on it, that reminded me of Felix the Cat. Then came the breathless moment. He stopped beside me, nodded his head, and said solemnly, 'Ach, Jah, she has fingers, too'. I had been accepted.

Berlin was, indeed, the mecca for all musicians. And for a young girl, passionately in love with music, they were halcyon days – days spent immersed in the culture and the civilization of a great city which had not yet begun to take on the undertones that lay just a few years ahead. Like a kaleidoscope, memories pass before my mind's eye. Life in the Pension Fink – which we called Finkenest – where students from all parts of the world found a home from home; being present, through an influential friend who was Lady-in-Waiting to the Kaiserin, at Royal Command Performances and Imperial celebrations; seated in the gallery of the private chapel of the Dome of Schloss watching the marriage ceremony of the Kaiser's second son; listening enraptured to the genius of such musicians as Pablo, de Sarsate, Nikish, Jacques Thibauld, Lilli Lehman, Gerhardt, Carreno, Ysaawe, Suggia, Casals, Schumann, Heink (for whom my uncle wrote and conducted an oratorio in New York), Pachmann, and many others; attending a never-to-be-forgotten spectacle of a military tournament at Templehof, at which the Kaiser and Kaiserin were present . . . . Those were my Berlin days and, interlarded with them, equally rapturous days spent amid the glistening snow of the Grunewald Forest; holidays in Dresden and the Hartz Mountains, a Christmas Eve celebrated in the rich, full tradition that belongs to Germany, and, above all else, practising the piano for six hours a day and spending six fruitful months learning the techniques of portrait painting.

Then a journey to London, there to mingle in the Members' Enclosure at Sandown Park, with Lillie Langtry, with Edward VII and other members of the royal family. It was my second visit to London. I had been there five years earlier with my parents and three brothers both to celebrate, with the rest of Britain, the relief of Mafeking and the Boer War Peace Proclamation, and to be present at a gathering of the Siedle clan – Siedles from Ceylon, Siedles from Durban and Siedles from Britain. We watched the procession along the Mall that preceded the coronation of the king; we sat entranced at the fireworks display held that same evening in the Crystal Palace and we drank in all the music and culture that London in those twilight days of peace could offer us.

Perla 1909, on holiday with her parents in Berlin.

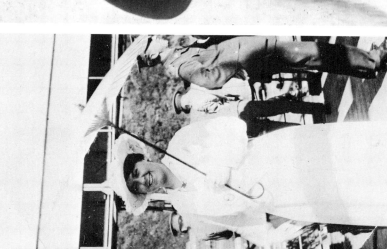

Perla 1915, mingling with Australian and New Zealand troops returning home *via* Durban after aborted Dardanelles campaign.

Perla 1908, in Austria.

Wedded to Jack Gibson September 1917.

Roy	Joy	Perla	Barrie
(1918)	(1921)		(1919)

This time Jack's got his hands full.

New York was our next stop. There we were met by my uncle – my father's brother, Edward Siedle – and his wife, Carrie. Uncle Edward was the technical director of the Metropolitan Opera House, and his wife was a renowned costume designer. As was the case everywhere else we had been, we 'did' the eastern seaboard of the United States thoroughly – Coney Island in company with Ted Siedle (a cousin of contemporary age), baseball games, swimming in the Hudson River, rowing in the St. Lawrence, fishing amid the Thousand Islands, and staring awestruck at the majesty of the Niagara Falls.

I returned to Durban to school and later my mother took me to Berlin. I remained there, studying music and painting until 1909, and then, torn between the sadness of leaving my Berlin friends and the tugging nostalgia of Durban and home, I sailed for South Africa. On 28 July of that year I made my musical debut in Durban's City Hall, situated, at that time, on the site where the Post Office now stands, and I revelled in the exhilaration that was accorded a 'home-town girl who had made good'. In the audience that night, though I was not to know until years later – was Jack Gibson, the man I was to marry.

Happy days followed – days filled with the warmth of close friends, of fun and games, of dancing parties, of music, riding and swimming and, above all, the intimacy of a closely-knit family together once again.

I was present in the following year as a representative of Natal at the pageant marking the birth of the Union of South Africa, and less than twelve months later I was in India with my mother visiting the Ceylon Siedles and again 'doing' the sights with the same enthusiasm and thoroughness that marked our other expeditions abroad.

Back in Durban we were living in Ludlow, a large, double-storeyed house with big garden, tennis court, croquet lawn, garages and stables, when, with tragic suddenness, our happiness was shattered by World War I – the Kaiser's war, we called it. To different theatres of fighting went my three grown-up brothers and my fiancé, Jack Gibson, and to this day I can recall the agony of watching from Ludlow's upstairs balcony first the ship of my brother Karl, and then my fiancé's ship disappear around the Bluff, headed for Europe and the bloodbath in which the world was locked. In 1915 Grandmother Watson died and we moved into an inherited Lynnville that was the fourth home the Siedle family occupied.

With the war raging and the family widely scattered, Jack, now commissioned in the Sixth Dragoon Guards, and in training for active duty in France, was recalled to join his father's wool-buying business in the Orange Free State; it being considered by the military powers-that-be that buying desperately needed wool constituted a great strategic necessity than adding one more name to the list of those missing or dead in France.

And so it was that Jack and I were married at Lynnville on 27 September 1917.

A success in his business, Jack built our home on the Berea and we called it Pineholme. It was a beautiful, rambling bungalow with a spacious music salon, and, in the years between the two world wars it was to become forever associated with the Siedle family. It was here from 1920 onwards there was maintained what was, in the accepted European sense of the word, a salon where music, the arts and the pure love of conversation were encouraged. Enshrined in the memories of Pineholme are many of the most famous names of the theatre, the concert hall and of literature.

By March 1918 a slump had hit the country and the wool-buying business collapsed. Pineholme, now complete, had to be rented, and we continued living in a beach bungalow

'PINEHOLME' – the Gibson home that features so much in the text

Joy Liddiard says: 'Throughout the war years 'Pineholme' was open-house to all Service men and women. (When I think about it none of them violated the privilege.) Those hundreds of men and women so valued the comfort, rest and temporary escape from the rigours of war that Pineholme offered them. But everybody in Durban felt blessed to be away from the bombing, rationing, and disruption to family life, and deemed it an honour to provide some little warmth to those who weren't so fortunate.

Our dining-room table could seat 20 with all its panels in place, but sometimes there were as many as forty in the house at one time. As a housewife today in England I realise only too well the cost of always being prepared for unexpected guests. I think our old Zulu cook had a secret weapon – always a great pot of home-made soup, plus unrestricted quantities of fruit and vegetables.

The servants were always told that if Mom or I were out, any uniformed caller, man or woman, should be invited to come in and wait. They'd be given a cold drink, tea or coffee, and whoever got home first was greeted with the news that there were visitors in the house or enjoying the 'coolth' of the garden.

We never counted heads but 'Pineholme' provided a warm spot in the hearts of many hundreds of Service visitors over the five years of war.'

'PINEHOLME' – two interior views

belonging to my father.

They were, in a sense, material losses which, Jack and I, both young, both infused with incurable optimism, knew we would one day retrieve. But on that 30 March came another blow. My mother was in the Lynnville garden, supervising the pruning of a bougainvilia hedge alongside an orange grove, when a cable was delivered to her. It stated baldly that my brother, Major K.O Siedle, MC, of the Royal Heavy Artillery, had been wounded at the Somme. Nothing more. My father sent frantic cables to every known contact he had abroad for further details, but before replies could be received from any one of them another – official – communication was received. Karl had been killed. It was all utterly inexplicable and a long time was to elapse before the full, tragic story was unfolded. In the midst of the big Somme offensive, Karl, hurrying his men into their dugouts, was wounded in the back and suffered a serious injury to his lung. He was taken to a Canadian field hospital at Gouzaincourt and was well enough to write us a postcard telling us of the misfortune that had befallen him. He was on the operating table when Germans bombed the hospital and Karl and many others were killed. The German excuse was that they believed the hospital to be a camouflaged munitions dump. The shock of Karl's death had a terrible effect on my mother, who had a heart attack, followed by a nervous breakdown, and for weeks she was close to death.

My husband, Jack, decided that he must rejoin the forces and he went with my brother Ted into the South African Artillery. Just at this time our first baby, Roy, was born into an atmosphere that could not have been sadder or more grim. My mother was desperately ill; I had become a victim of double-septic pneumonia, known as 'Spanish Flu', and for two months my life hung in the balance and all the men in the family, except my father, were away on active service.

But the war finally drew to its close and on Armistice Day nurses helped my mother and me on to the balcony of Lynnville. We sat there sobbing, helplessly weak, listening to the chorus of church bells as they rang out to proclaim the end of the war.

Then began the long, slow task of rebuilding our world.

My Mother's heart was so bad that it was no longer advisable that she continue living in double-storeyed Lynnville. Fortunately, Pineholme was available again, so my father bought it and into it they moved, there to remain for the rest of their lives.

I had, before the war, set out to be a pianist, but is was singing that eventually was to prove my forte. How it happened is another of those twists of fate which so often were to change the ordered course of my life. In 1909, back from Berlin, I met Mr. Norman Salmond, the Leeds Festival Singer, who had come to live in Durban for health reasons. Quite naturally, his major preoccupation in life was singing, and it transpired, in due course, that I had, in his view, 'quite a voice'. But it was only after the First World War had broken out that I dared to sing in public – and then only in the West Street canteen where troops were entertained while they awaited the ships that would take them to the battlefields. From the platform I sang all the rollicking marching songs and the other favourites of that period. History was to repeat itself a generation later as events were to prove, but no such thought could have been further from my mind as I stood urging the troops to join in the choruses of 'It's a Long Long Way to Tipperary', 'Home, Sweet Home', and the other equally popular tunes of those days. I, even in that war, sang a farewell to two troopships, the *Mersey* and the *Trent*, never dreaming that this was to be the forerunner of an event which a generation later would become part of the daily routine of my life. I was on the bridge of the tug which had the *Mersey* in tow, and as the moment came to cast off the hawser, Captain Rainnie, the tug master handed me his megaphone and said 'What about giving them a song before they leave?'

I did. They all joined in the choruses and a rich volume of sound came rolling across to us on that still, blue morning. Some time later a heavy package was delivered to me by the Navy. In it was a paperweight made from a piece of the *Mersey*'s gun shield which had been blackened and twisted from a direct hit in an encounter with the German naval vessel, the *Koenigsberg*. Engraved on the paperweight were these words:

'Koenigsberg – Mersey
To Miss Perla Siedle as an appreciation of her kindness
to the Mersey and Trent crews on their departure.'

It is still on my desk to this day.

Some time later I was in London with my three young children and I met Stephan Mavrogodarto, a voice specialist. He asked to hear me sing as he feared that, without proper scientific training, I had damaged my vocal chords by singing operas and oratorios in which, by now, I had become fairly accomplished. After hearing me, he pronounced a verdict which, while it was the one I was longing to hear, nevertheless brought in its train complex domestic problems. I was in London with three small children and back in South Africa was my husband, Jack. I wrote both to him and to my parents. Not unexpectedly my parents, wildly enthusiastic about anything musical, gave the project – Mavrogodarto had suggested that I undergo a full course in singing – their full support. More cautiously, Jack suggested a three-month trial. So I rented a house and engaged a trained nurse for the children and started my daily lessons with Mavrogodarto in London, subsequently specializing in Italian arias, in Wagner, in oratorio with Sir Henry Wood and with the Covent Garden Wagnerian coach, Hermann Grunebaum.

My three months with Mavrogodarto were to stretch into two and a half years, with the first eight months devoted solely to vowels – I never sang a song in that time – until he had satisfied himself with the quality of every note throughout my range. Over the remaining period I built up a wide repertoire of songs based on the sound foundation of music which I already had and I took, of course, advantage of every possible opportunity to attend song recitals and concerts.

In due course I made my first public appearance as a singer and received, as Sir Henry Wood put it, my 'London hall-mark' from the critics. Then followed many public appearances including one at which I represented South Africa in celebration of South Africa Day. The invitation came from Lady Buxton, who had organized the concert under the distinguished patronage of Prince and Princess Arthur of Connaught.

Mavrogodarto's technique in training was what is known as 'open-throat' singing, in which the voice is unfettered by any extraneous muscular effort or contraction of the throat. Many, many years later, when dockside singing had become for me my self-appointed daily chore, musicians were horrified at the consequences this would have and some warned that my voice wouldn't last a week under such rigorous conditions. I, of course, disregarded their warnings and continued with outdoor singing, believing that if I were to lose my voice then that loss could be offset against those years of fulfillment as 'The Lady in White'. My voice, however, never once failed, and only a few months ago, when a throat specialist examined me, he said that despite the years and years of singing out of doors my vocal chords were completely unimpared – nothing short of a miracle, in his view.

Perla 1923. Her debut at a Durban concert.

Perla 1933. At a concert in Johannesburg.

—— 3 ——

The joyous years

And so, as I have said, we went back to Pineholme, there to take up again the threads of the life we had known and loved so well. What a wonderful sense of belonging to step across a familiar threshold into an atmosphere of warm, friendly hospitality, to embrace again the well-being derived as an intimate and loved part of a closely-knit and devoted family. There was the broad, polished verandah on which one could stand and gaze across graceful, shady palm trees and ferns to the harbour; there the salon, dominated by the grand piano around which we as a family had so often gathered to sing and laugh together; there the large lofty rooms, dark polished floors covered with exquisite rugs, warmly coloured portraits and paintings adorning the walls; there the lovely carved antique tables, the Chinese cabinets, the heavy bronze and copper works of art that had once held incense in Chinese and Indian temples – all fitting harmoniously into a pattern of peace and contentment.

The years between the world wars were to see the blossoming of our family life in Pineholme to its fullest – years into which were crammed all the diverse activities – sport, music, art, welfare, literary discussions and musical get-togethers – to one or other of which members of the family, depending on their particular enthusiasms, devoted themselves energetically and wholeheartedly.

They were full and rewarding years, indeed, in which (if anything could be said to take precedence over anything else) music predominated. 'Visitors must think us music mad – father, mother, children – all inveterate fans', my father once remarked. Our taste for music was cultivated from the earliest days when we, as very small children, would cluster round the piano to sing nursery rhymes and folk-songs. My four brothers, Karl, Basil, Ted and Jack, apparently not content with the melodic output of a mere piano, devised stringed instruments, using cigar boxes and violin strings fixed into biscuit tins to provide the necessary sound amplification. Using bows they played these improvised 'cellos and succeeded in extracting from them fascinating, if reedy, notes. As the years went by Jack and Karl both became accompished 'cellists and played in the Durban civic orchestra.

Cricketing, like music, was in our family's blood. To my brother, Jack, it was an obsession, and when he had sons of his own he trained them to love the sport with the same devotion that he had displayed. I have a sports magazine recording the fact that in one cricket match there were four Siedles – my brother Jack and his three sons.

All my four brothers also played inter-town and inter-provincial rugby and for eleven years in succession there was one, and sometimes two, Siedles in these teams. My brother Karl, a powerful all-rounder, has his memory as a sportsman enshrined in the stone clock tower that dominates the twelve playing-fields at Kingsmead. It was erected in his honour – after his death in France – by his fellow club-members.

Basil was another 'international', playing for the Springboks against the All Blacks in New Zealand. My remaining brother, Ted, who was a fine swimmer and played inter-town rugby, found that the needs of his farm left him with little opportunity for sport, but his enthusiasm for it remained undimmed.

Even I was caught up in the infectious enthusiasm for

cricket and would bowl, in our garden, to a makeshift side composed of my brothers and sons of our neighbour, Dr. Sam Campbell. Roy Campbell one of those sons, was destined to be one of the three greatest English poets of his era.

For my brothers these garden games had a memorable sequel. Jack played for South Africa against Lord Tennyson's touring team in 1924–5; he toured England with a South African side in 1929 and 1935 and was selected as vice-captain of the team to tour Australia in 1931–2. He was, however, unable to accompany the team on this occasion.

He opened for South Africa on 22 occasions and held the record opening stand, with Bruce Mitchell, of 260 against England at Cape Town in the 1930–1 Test series. In the 1935 tour of England he was the first player to achieve 1,000 runs. He had been running neck and neck with Herbert Sutcliffe and it was in Yorkshire that he triumphantly chalked up his 1,000th run. His cricketing prowess received its final accolade when, in 1963, he was elected an honorary life member of the MCC.

My love of the docks, too, was a deeply ingrained family instinct. On Sundays, as a very small child, I was frequently taken to the harbour by my father and as often as not wound up sitting on the knee of some bewhiskered sea captain while incomprehensible nautical affairs were being talked about around me. I loved the tall ships, rocking at their moorings; the bustling activities of the harbour itself and the sight of sailors from far-off, exotic lands. The docks, of course, were to grow out of all recognition during my lifetime, but, for me, they never lost their fascination.

In his early days my father used to walk to the docks along a sandy, dusty road, but in due time 'civilization', in the form of a tram service, was introduced and access to the docks was made easier.

As a family we used to travel around Durban in a handsome carriage and pair which was later superseded by a motor-car, my father being among the first in Durban to own one of these newfangled 'horseless carriages'.

School holidays were joyous occasions, devoted in the main to exploring the country of our birth, travelling extensively through it by taking advantage of my father's close links with shipping and my mother's widely scattered family living on farms in various beautiful areas of South Africa. We came to know all the coastal ports from Durban to Cape Town – I can still remember sacks of oysters being hauled over the ship's sides and our sitting around on the deck while the chief officer, with his jack-knife, opened the shells for us. Lourenço Marques, with its exotic 'continental' atmosphere, had a particular appeal for us, as children. We would breakfast at 11 – it was nearly always served with wine – and spend the days enjoying the sights of the city, peopled with gaily uniformed officials, and attending, on occasions, bullfights; tame affairs then as compared with the present day.

Our farm holidays were totally different but equally fascinating – swimming in icy mountain streams, trout-fishing, ox-wagon picnics and riding and climbing up to the mountain caves to examine Bushman rock-paintings.

As I think back over the full life that we led at Pineholme what celebrity-studded memories come vividly to life. I see them again in the music salon of Pineholme, entertaining and being entertained. All the arts – music, literature, theatre, painting – represented at one time or another by the leading luminaries in their spheres – May Mukle, the 'cellist, Marie Hall, the violinist, Sir Granville Bantock, the composer, Count John McCormack, Clara Butt, Matheson Lang, Sybil Thorndike, Yehudi Menuhin, Solomon, Hiefetz, Moiseowitch, Sir Frank Benson, H.B. Irving, Carreno,

Kennerly Rumford, Vaughan Thomas, Gustave Hallé, Freda Godfrey, Leonard Rayne, Joseph Hislop, Elsie Hall, Claudio Arrau, Esta d'Argo, Noel Eadie, Ada Forrest, Cherry Kearton, Betsy de la Porte, Cecelia Wessels, Lady Blackwell, with whom I gave many lieder recitals, and Hugh Tracey. Then there were the conductors Theo Wendt, William Pickerill, Charles Webber, of the D'Oyly Carte Company, and the Durban musical directors with whom I worked, R.H. McDonald, Charles Hoby, Frank Proudman, Lyell-Taylor, Dan Godfrey and Edward Dunn.

There are four more names to be added – of literary giants – but of them more must be told than a mere mention of their names for the impact they made was profound. Two of them were fellow Durbanites of mine, Roy Campbell and Noel Langley, and the other two were George Bernard Shaw and Douglas Reed.

It was at a concert in May 1935, in the Durban City Hall, that I met Bernard Shaw and his wife. They were paying their first visit to South Africa and were spending some time in Durban. In the first half of the programme I had sung 'Rebecca's Prayer' from *Ivanhoe* and was more than a little surprised during the interval to receive a message saying that Bernard Shaw had expressed a wish to meet me.

I shall never forget that night. He was with his wife in the foyer talking to Dan Godfrey, the musical director. He looked at me with those penetrating blue eyes of his and then took my breath away by saying: 'What are you doing here?' I started to give him a halting 'Oh, but you asked to see me . . .', when he cut me short.

'I mean, what are you doing singing in this godforsaken hole when you could take your place in the front rank of any continental concert platform?' He said: 'You are a Brünhilde and can sing Wagner's Liebstod, of course? It is like falling off a stool to you.'

'Not quite,' I replied, 'but I have sung it before with the Durban civic orchestra on several occasions.'

He told me that he had heard it in London when it was performed there for the first time and that he had never heard anything like it before.

With that he began to describe the Liebestod and its unexpected cadences of key. I was astounded by his knowledge of music, forgetting at the time that for many years he had been one of London's leading art and music critics. He asked me whether, as a special favour, I would sing in the second half of the programme his wife's favourite song 'Who Is Sylvia'. I said I would be delighted. After the concert the Shaw's invited me to the hotel where they were staying and again I was to be enthralled by his phenomenal knowledge of music. A close friendship grew between the Shaws and the Siedle clan, with Shaw insisting on addressing me as 'Perlissima'.

At Pineholme in the intimacy of the warm hospitality that surrounded him, the dramatist told us eloquently and wittily of incidents in his life. In particular, I recall his account of his days as an art critic, when he met Epstein. The sculptor boasted to Shaw: 'I am considered the greatest living sculptor in stone.' To which Shaw retorted: 'You are, are you? Well go and apprentice yourself to a stone mason and when you can carve a decent kerbstone, let me know.'

On another occasion Shaw, in whom the art critic was anything but dormant, closely examined my paintings that hung on the walls commenting: 'The arts are so closely wedded that one is conscious of the rhythm of your music in your painting and the colour of your painting in your music.'

The Shaws often joked about their marriage. Mrs. Shaw said that she had to marry him because he had had a bicycle accident and didn't have the foggiest idea of looking after himself, to which Shaw retorted: 'I nearly lost her at the altar. I wore my shabbiest suit for the wedding while my best man was looking immaculate. The parson thought that he was the groom and almost married her off to him, but I managed to stop him in time.' Mrs. Shaw added: 'And he chose our honeymoon in which to write *The Life of Wagner*.'

Shaw left me some delightful mementoes of his visit. One is a set of photographs of himself, on each of which he wrote his own caption. On the first, a picture of him as a comparatively young man with a neatly trimmed beard, he wrote: 'You will hardly believe it, but I used to resemble this slightly vulgar person.' On the next, one looking up in surprise from his desk, the caption reads: 'The interrupted inspiration. What the devil is the matter *now*?' The third, the famous portrait of a benign Bernard Shaw, with his right eyebrow protruding, he captioned: 'This is the pious author of *St. Joan*. The man with the white eyebrow.' The final photograph – Shaw as an old man – has this comment: 'I can grin as idiotically as anybody when I want to look harmless.' Other photographs bear such remarks as: 'Who says I am not hardworking?', 'In profile the Public Man', and one bearing the laconic word 'Grandpa'. With the letter accompanying the photographs Shaw wrote: 'My dear Perla: I have just dug out this old collection from a neglected corner of my writing case. They are all "comparatively youthful", but my present aspect is "unbearable" Affectionately, GBS'

He also added his contribution – a sort of tabloid autobiography – to my autograph book. It read:

> 'G. Bernard Shaw
> Limited baritone
> Had to take to literature
> Would never have written a line if

He had a voice like Perlissima's
Wanted to be a great painter
Would have been if he had Perlissima's fingers
Some people have all the luck
Wasted on silly Durban
How conceited that woman must be!
                                22nd May, 1935.'

Bernard Shaw was 79 when I met him and he was at his most irreverent, delighting in upsetting existing shibboleths. As he breezed through South Africa he left behind him a trail of iconoclastic quotations that set up a furore in a section of the population and its Press. 'Your Natives here', he said, 'are better mannered than your whites and many of them are more efficient.'

'Intermarriage is the solution to racial and colour problems.'

'Sunshine in South Africa keeps the European birth-rate low.'

'I like South Africa, but it is the sort of country you cannot get a living out of unless you put chemicals into it.'

'Your Afrikaners are a fine people physically but they keep running away from civilization. I wish someone would make them realize that the Bible is a well-written book but that it should be supplemented with Whittaker.'

Roy Campbell was a frequent and much loved visitor to Pineholme, and we, of course, followed with deep interest filming of *Pickwick Papers*, which he was directing. I was amazed at his mastery of the entire complex operation and his infinite patience in repeating rehearsal after rehearsal until his perfectionist nature was appeased. Now living in Hollywood, I still receive from him letters that sparkle with all his old wit and personality. He felt, he told me in one of his letters, a yearning nostalgia for the land of his birth, but

Hollywood had to remain his 'material home'.

'I often feel like a cormorant,' he wrote, 'the tame bird that catches the fat fish, only in my case it is taken away from me by the tax man.'

Douglas Reed, author of *Insanity Fair* and those other dramatically prophetic books of the shape of things to come, was a post-war visitor to Pineholme. It was in the house I now occupy at 250, Chelmsford Road, Berea, that he wrote what he described as his first moderately successful novel *Reasons of Health*, and he also started there his last but one, political travel book, *Somewhere South of Suez*. He thereby doubly qualifies for mention as a literary luminary within the Siedle orbit.

He has written nothing for years because, he told me, if he continued to be a political writer all he could write would be 'Insanity Fairs' for the rest of his days.

'I spent years of despondency in Germany watching the "Unnecessary War" approach. They were followed by even worse years – those of wartime in England – for I saw from 1941 onwards that the war was not being truly fought for the causes proclaimed to "the people", and that its issue would be a situation worse and more pregnant with another unnecessary war than was the case in the period 1933–9.

'Sick at heart I wanted only to turn my back on the places where I had been forced to watch the locusts eat the years. I wanted to breathe a different air and that was how I came to South Africa – to Durban, and to 250, Chelmsford Road, in March 1948.

'For a writer it was the perfect home and the balcony or the little room at the end of it when the wind blew too hard for the paper to remain in my typewriter were the best places I have known.

'And when I was still a writer I knew many places:
I wrote a book in a room in Vienna; in an hotel in
Prague – both these were interrupted by the noise of
Hitler's invasion; on a balcony in Budapest; in a
basement room – where the light seldom entered – in
Montreal; in a 70th floor cubbyhole in New York; and in
many other locales, some good, some poor, but the best
of them not to compare with that high seat in Durban
where the city and the harbour lay spread beneath me –
night and day.'

If Douglas Reed doesn't write any more, he does
occasionally produce little rhymes for his own private
pleasure and that of his family. I recall a rhyme he wrote in
my book at Pineholme:

'I met a man and shook his hand
And said, "You're great, it's simply grand
To meet you." With extended paw
He said: "I'm very pleased, I'm Shaw."
'I always felt I autolaph when I inscribe by autograph
Among great one like that no less! of John Bull's only
    GBS.
"A poor thing" said my teacher erst, when tediously I
    scrawled it first.
'And ever since it's been the same; a very poorly
    written name.
It never grew to big stature, this silly little signature
It looks as if, I truly think, it had been reared on
    rationed ink.
'For nevertheless, I must bequeath the one that
    genuflects beneath
To Perla, Lady-famed-in-white, her friendship and
    Gastfreundlichkeit.

I'll never Pine for Holme indeed, while I can meet such friends in need. In gratitude from Douglas Reed. 1948'

In World War II I was to come into contact with many men who had been blinded in battle and I never ceased to be amazed how most of them, in time, adjusted to their handicap and were able to take life in full stride again. To Pineholme, in those early days, there came Alfred Hollins, the famous organist, who was totally blind and one of the most remarkable men I have ever met in my life.

He visited South Africa twice, and on both occasions he stayed as our guest at Pineholme. He had been blind from birth, but from the confident, easy way in which he moved around it was almost impossible to realize that he was unable to see. Shown once over the house by my father, he seemed to know every inch of it and from then on would come, almost dancing, down the stairs with only his fingers lightly brushing the banisters. He meticulously kept a diary, making entries in it each evening with a typewriter which he used with speed and skill.

His second visit to South Africa – in 1916 – was to supervise the installation of an organ in the Johannesburg City Hall – destined to be one of the biggest organs ever built, with a weight of more than 60 tons. It had 10 miles of pneumatic piping and 6,532 pipes, some of them so large that a small boy could crawl through them. The skins of 532 sheep were used for the wind reservoirs and valves. After supervising its installation – it was ordered in 1913, but took three years to complete – Alfred Hollins gave the opening recital on it and several other concerts before coming to Durban. I had been delegated to meet him at the station and the family briefing included the strict injunction not to use the word 'see'. I arrived at the station driving the huge eight-seater family Daimler and had my initial surprise. He was alone. He had neither companion nor valet with him. The very first request he made was to 'see' the organ in the Durban City Hall into which new stops had been fitted. This involved a very close and careful fingering of its keyboard and stops and then the playing of it.

Then he wanted to 'see' a cricket match – 'haven't seen one in ages', he declared – and I took him to the match at which my parents were present as organizers.

During his stay in Durban he composed three songs for me to sing to the audience attending the organ recital he gave in the City Hall. Equally brilliant as a pianist, he accompanied me as I sang. On the evening of the concert – in those expansive days full evening dress was *de rigueur* – my father went up to his room to inquire if he could help him dress and was surprised to find his room in total darkness. Switching on the light my father found him immaculately attired in tails, his bow-tie perfectly tied, and busy putting the finishing touches to his toilet.

In addition to a remarkable memory he had extremely sensitive hands and feet. Returning to a ship in which he had travelled several years previously he said to the captain: 'I see you have a new carpet.' Surprised, the captain confessed he hadn't noticed it himself, but on checking with the purser it transpired that a new carpet had, in fact, been fitted before the ship sailed on its previous voyage.

4

War

Britain was at war with Germany.

As far as South Africa was concerned the immediate future was obscure, for a tense political situation had developed that was to be resolved at a special session of Parliament following a Cabinet meeting at the Prime Minister's residence, Groote Schuur, on Sunday, 3 September. For two days we sat with our ears glued to the radio, debating, analysing and pondering on the incredible situation that had arisen. Throughout the country eager young men were clamouring for an immediate delaration of war against Germany and mobilization, but behind the locked doors of the Cabinet room General Smuts was fighting the grimmest political battle of his career. Parliament met on Monday, 4 September, and at exactly 9.10 that night came the fateful announcement that General Smuts had won the debate in Parliament by a mere thirteen votes. We were at war.

While young men in every city and town in the country rushed to join up, we, in Durban, of the Women's Auxiliary of the Seamen's Institute, with memories of the First World War, began organizing the dockside canteen which we knew would be needed just as soon as the ships with their crammed cargoes of fighting men and material started to call at Durban on their way to the far-flung theatres of war.

Fortuitously, some time before the war the Seamen's Institute had planned to erect a dockside canteen for merchant seamen, so it was merely a matter of adapting these plans to a greater need. My mother had picked the site for the building and by April 1940 the canteen was ready. Five days later the first Rhodesian troops passed through Durban for Mombasa. In time, we were to find that the new canteen was totally inadequate to cope with the demand made upon it and two mobile canteens were later introduced.

The excitement of active war touched Durban fleetingly as our preparations were going ahead for the establishment of the canteen. France had capitulated and Italy – Mussolini with his contemptible 'stab in the back' – had declared was on her prostrate neighbour. In Durban at that time were two Italian ships, the *Gerusaleme* and the *Timavo*, which immediately made a dash for neutral territory – the closest being Lourenço Marques, a dependency of Portugal. The fleeing ships were promptly chased by the British armed merchantmen *Ranchi* and *Carthage*, and by the South African Air Force. The *Timavo* had reached a point known as Leadsmen's Shoal, about 160 miles from Durban, when a SAAF Junkers swept out of the sky and attacked her. The panicky Italian crew beached their vessel, the remains of which can be seen to this day. The *Gerusaleme* made Lourenço Marques safely, and there she remained until the defeat of Italy, when she was handed over to the British authorities and converted into a hospital ship.

I later did a painting of the *Gerusaleme*, being permitted to do so by a special concession granted by the authorities provided it was submitted for their scrutiny before anyone else was allowed to see it.

Rigid security regulations were clamped on Durban harbour. Barbed wire fences were hurriedly thrown up to cut it off from all but those officially authorized to come and go; submarine nets spanned the harbour entrance and armed sentries patrolled the perimeters and stood watch over the gates. As canteen workers, we were issued with

The RN Association shield being presented to The Lady-in-White on her 80th birthday, by Commanders Creswell, Carter and Wingrove.

My utmost Respects for the job you are doing —
photographer Denis Lucey
HMS VANGUARD 1947

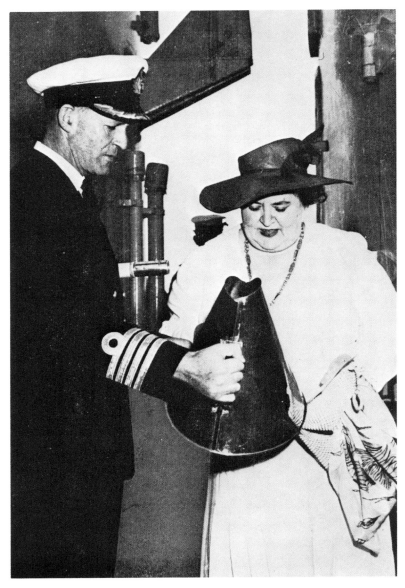

Presented, on board *HMS Nigeria*, with the burnished copper – Mark 3–megaphone. Making the presentation is Captain Scott. (see page 68.)

special passes which, while they gained us entry to the dock area, entitled us to no information whatever about the pending arrival and departure of convoys. It was thus impossible to plan in advance what quantities of food would be required, but we were able in a short time to overcome this difficulty simply by appealing to the generosity of Durban. Unlike other countries at war, South Africa was suffering from no real shortages of anything, but more important, a generous population was prepared at all time to share what they had willingly whenever called upon to do so. It had merely to become known that a large convoy was in port before food, cigarettes and other soldier 'comforts' poured into our canteen for distribution. I do not think there was a family in Durban which had not, before the war ended, adopted at least a dozen soldiers, sailors and airmen to whom they regularly sent food parcels.

The first South Africans to leave for East Africa sailed in the four-funnelled ship *Takliwa* on 10 April 1940. They were the South African Reconnaisance Unit and, with the precedent now established when I sang goodbye to the Rhodesian troops, I sang to these soldiers too, who were to be the first South Africans to go on active service in World War II. Twenty years later I was to receive a letter from Major W.C. Griffiths who was on board the *Takliwa*. 'Amid the hubbub of calling the roll and the multifarious duties connected with the embarkation of troops and stores', he wrote, 'the strong voice of a lady dressed in white was heard singing *Pack Up Your Troubles* and all the 1914–18 songs that thrilled and remain so dear to British troops. 'That voice was yours – the voice that made you and Durban famous with the Allied forces. Your singing linked the thoughts of those men on that 8,000-ton troopship with the dear ones left behind.'

The *Delwara* was a vessel which was to carry the first big contingent of South African troops to East Africa, but I sang no song of farewell to her. On board were my two sons, Roy, aged 21, and Barrie, 20, members of the First Transvaal Scottish. I was afraid to sing. I would have broken down. I had not yet developed the inner strength which in the years ahead were to sustain me when faced with moments that seemed emotionally unbearable.

There was tremendous excitement and activity on the day – 17 July 1940 – that the *Delwara* sailed. Crowds of civilians stood behind the barbed-wire enclosures at the harbour to watch the heavily laden soldiers march up the gangway of the *Delwara* and the other ships of the convoy, cheering wildly as they recognized this or that unit. Within a few hours the black ships had sunk lower in the water and from every porthole, from every inch of deck space and from every part of the rigging no matter how precarious, soldiers jostled each other and waved and shouted to the crowds beyond the barbed-wire fences.

Many men who left that day were to earn renown on the battlefields of East Africa, the Western Desert and Italy and some were not to come back – my son Roy among them.

The South African Expeditionary Force, small though it was, and composed entirely of volunteers, was to achieve one of the most remarkable campaign victories in the history of the war – one which I believe has not received anything like the recognition it deserves. Advancing from Kenya, the Allied forces, of which the South Africans constituted an integrated, highly mobile spearhead, totally defeated the entire strength of the Italian army opposed to them. This southern force, together with the northern force, killed or captured virtually every single white Italian soldier; the Regia Aeronautica of Ethiopia was destroyed; the hundreds of thousands of Italian colonial troops, well disciplined and armed, were so utterly defeated that, their morale shattered, the survivors abandoned their uniforms to slink back with their arms to the safe anonymity of the African bush. The enemy's vastly superior artillery strength was discounted by the ingenuity with which the South Africans turned to advantage the rugged African terrain in which they were fighting. Supplies, medical stores and other equipment of such astronomical quantities as to be beyond accurate assessment fell into Allied hands. According to Brigadier 'Scrubbs' Hartshorn, who commanded the First Transvaal Scottish in the Abyssinian campaign, of that vast enemy force of 300,000 men, detailed to preserve Mussolini's East African Empire, not a man, with the possible exception of a handful of senior officers, survived to take up arms against the Allied forces in the Western Desert or elsewhere during the remainder of World War II. In the whole of the East African campaign the South African land forces casualties were 270 men, including 73 killed.

Later in the war I was to meet 'Scrubbs' Hartshorn, a dynamic, soldierly-looking man, one-armed, with an infectious laugh and a uniform emblazoned with ribbons from the First World War, to receive his thanks for an odd gift I was instrumental in providing. At the beginning of the East African campaign when the troops were poorly equipped, 'Scrubbs' Hartshorn had cabled an appeal for help to buy 'kaffir' pots, the three-legged iron containers, which, in Africa, fulfil virtually all the functions of a whole range of kitchen utensils. I reacted immediately to such a typically South African appeal and arranged for one of my paintings, a great splash of flamboyance, to be auctioned, the resulting funds to be devoted to buying the 'kaffir' pots.

'Scrubbs' Hartshorn, in Durban in the course of a morale-raising tour of the country, asked to see my studio and pictures – he proved most knowledgeable about paintings and, since the war's end, has to his credit many outstanding oils of African scenes painted despite the handicap of one arm. In a momentary silence, as we stood alone, he put his arm around my shoulders and spoke gently of my son Roy, killed in Italy, and then he said suddenly: 'Now you must sing better than ever. You have created a place for yourself as one of the leaders of our war effort. You are making friends for us among our Allies before we on the field ever meet them.'

Among those who sailed on the *Delwara* was South Africa's first team of war correspondents, among them Carel Birkby, Conrad Norton, Uys Krige, and the singer Bruce Anderson, who was with a broadcasting recording unit. Uys Krige and Con Norton were to spend many years in Italian and German prisoner-of-war camps after their capture at Sidi Rezegh in 1941, and it was only after his release at the war's end that Con Norton was to tell me of a dramatic incident that occurred when the *Delwara* was a few days out of Durban.

A day or so out from Durban the convoy of ships, of which the *Delwara* was one, was passing through an area where a pack of U-boats was known to be operating. It was a glorious, sunlit day, with the deep blue of the sea crisscrossed with a foaming white pattern from the threshing propellers of the escorting cruiser ceaselessly manoeuvring in, out and around the long lines of ships as they steamed steadily northwards. It was a day that seemed in no way different than had been spent so far but on the *Delwara* a drama was being enacted. A 19-year-old South African soldier lay in the sick bay stricken with spinal meningitis. His only hope of survival lay in his being administered, without delay, the correct drug. None was available on board.

On the bridge a South African military doctor argued earnestly, desperately, with the captain of the troopship. Signal the other ships in the convoy, he pleaded, in case they had the drug. The captain was adamant. It was strictly forbidden to break wireless silence under any circumstances. But the doctor refused to accept this and the argument raged to and fro until finally the captain consented to flash by heliograph a message to the cruiser. Back came answering flashes and soon the foredeck of the *Delwara* was alive with activity as sailors, armed with long boat-hooks, clambered over the side and hung from ropes, the boat-hooks extended. Above them an officer with field-glasses kept his eyes fixed on the cruiser which by now had swing round and was headed for a point directly ahead of the *Delwara*'s bows. 'There it goes', yelled the officer, and, with straining eyes, those in the *Delwara* scanned the sea now wildly threshing in the wake of the cruiser, which once again had swung around and was heading back to its position at the head of the convoy. Then they saw it. A white lifebelt bobbing in the water. Tied to it was a red Craven A cigarette tin in which lay the drug that spelt life or death for the unconscious soldier. Nearer and nearer floated the lifebelt to the *Delwara*, which by now had reduced speed to the point that it hardly seemed to be moving. The sailors strained their boat-hooks outwards. Those on deck strained in sympathy. Closer bobbed the lifebelt, within inches of one of the hooks. Then it floated away again, only to be flicked back into range by some white-winged wavelets that happened along. Again the hooks strained outwards, and then, as if tired of the tantalizing game being played, the lifebelt suddenly slipped sideways and, as if propelled by some unseen motor, it floated parallel with the ship, but out of range of the boat-hooks. The tragic end to the drama was being written, it seemed, in the white flurries and eddies that caressed the lifebelt as it floated on the sea.

But on the bridge the docter and captain were at it again. Lower a boat, demanded the doctor. Impossible, replied the harassed captain. It would mean stopping the ship – a court-martial offence. Precious seconds were passing as the agonized argument continued. The doctor, an Afrikaans-speaking South African, pleaded, threatened, implored, until the captain, torn between a lifetime's discipline and his own emotions gave the order that while possibly saving the life of one young, unknown soldier, lying unconscious in the sick-bay, could conceivably jepoardize the lives of thousands of soldiers entrusted to his care.

The *Delwara* bobbed gently in the waves, as, with incredible speed, a boat dropped into the water and seemed hardly to have done so before it was again being hoisted aboard with the officer in it tightly holding in his hand the precious red tin box. The *Delwara*'s engines throbbed again and soon – so incredibly short a time it seemed, for a life-and-death drama to have been enacted – it was back in place in the convoy steaming imperturbably onwards.

The soldier recovered. Con Norton visited him in Mombasa, where he was blissfully unaware of the drama that had been played out with his life at stake.

Soon after normality had returned on board the *Delwara* the war correspondents were called to the captain's cabin and there, with the doctor present, were told of the consequences that could ensue if the incident were to be publicly disclosed. No Admiralty Court would ever countenance the action of a captain endangering his ship, and indeed the whole convoy, to save the life of a single man.

With both our sons fighting in East Africa and with the fortunes of the Allies in other theatres steadily, and depressingly, deteriorating I detected a restlessness in my husband, Jack. He did what I knew he would one day do. He walked into a recruiting office, gave his age as 44 – conveniently lopping off ten years – and ended up in the South African Air Force. He was in Egypt a few months later, a member of No. 2 South African Fighter Squadron and known as 'Herman' because of his impressive row of medals from the First World War. When No. 2 Squadron arrived in Egypt from Kenya it brought with it the distinction – though that is hardly the right word – of having nearly shot down the aircraft in which Field-Marshall Smuts, Commander-in-Chief of the South African forces, was travelling.

General Smuts, on a tour of the front line in Kenya, was seated in the second pilot's seat of a Junkers bomber piloted by Captain Raubenheimer, of No. 12 Squadron, flying towards the oasis of Wajir where the South Africans were camped. In General Smuts aircraft were the top of the top brass; General Dickinson, British GOC, Sir Pierre van Ryneveld, Chief of the South African General Staff, General Godwen Austen, Brigadier Daniel, Chief of the South African Air Force, and other lesser lights, though not one below the rank of a full colonel. In an accompanying bomber were four war correspondents and various staff officers. As the aircraft, which was being escorted by Hurricanes, flew over a fighter airfield below, the occupants of the two bombers watched with interest as two fighters took off and headed straight for them, in what they surmised was to be a salute of welcome to the Commander-in-Chief. Their interest hurriedly changed to alarm as first one and then the other fighter went, quite obviously into attack manoeuvre, and seconds later bullets ripped through the fuselage of the aircraft in which General Smuts was travelling, one of the bullets missing him by inches. One of the fighters, recognizing the markings on the bombers, made off, but the other, more determined, returned to the attack.

Con Norton, in the accompanying bomber, who later told my that his sense of insecurity was heightened considerably by the fact that he was sitting on a box of live ammunition, saw the fighter again approach General Smut's plane, which by now was 'wagging' its wings wildly as a means of recognition, while the pilot had his fingers on his machine-guns ready to shoot down the fighter if it persisted in its mistaken idea that the bombers were enemy. Fortunately the fighter suddenly broke off and the bombers continued their journey. It was a General Smuts, livid with rage, who stepped from the aircraft at the next stopping point. Though in time the mistake of the fighter pilots was satisfactorily explained away and the squadron completely exonerated, General Smuts's concern was for the disastrous political consequences that could have ensued in South Africa – already deeply divided on the war issue – if he had been killed in such circumstances.

In Durban only my daughter Joy was left with me now that my husband Jack had gone north. I realized how my mother had felt in the First World War when my three brothers had all joined up and left for the German South West African campaign. But Joy, too, was restless and wanted in some way to do her share, but we agreed that she should not volunteer for overseas duty, so she joined the women's army, being stationed with a transport unit at the huge Imperial transit camp that was set up at Clairwood, just outside Durban. The reason for the camp was to permit troops, bound for the Far East, to spend some days on land instead of remaining on board the troopships in Durban harbour as had been the case up till then.

Whenever the South African troopships left I was, of course, there to sing them goodbye. The most sentimental send-off, as far as Durban was concerned, was that accorded the Durban Light Infantry which, under the command of Colonel Butler-Porter, sailed in the *Ile de France* on 10 June 1941. The South African Broadcasting Corporation, anxious to obtain a record of the now well-known musical send-offs to the troops, brought a recording van to the docks and I was asked to encourage the departing soldiers to sing with me. Try as I might they wouldn't sing. They were leaving their home town and emotions were too strong. I was to find later in the war that with incoming troopships no such reluctance to sing arose, but that with ships departing on what in almost every case was the last lap of the journey to the battlefield the troops preferred to listen rather than to join in. There were exceptions, of course, as with those ships which had formed choirs aboard to help while away the tedium of the long sea voyages. These choirs, usually composed of Welshmen, sang lustily with me on every possible occasion.

With the smashing South African victories in Abyssinia still a thrilling memory, the very thought of a defeat hardly entered out consciousness in those days. But South Africa was to suffer two major reverses in quick succession – Sidi Rezegh, on 23 November 1941, when the Fifth South African Brigade was practically destroyed, and then, in the following June, the fall of Tobruk, with the capture of 25,000 men, a large proportion of whom were South African.

But even in adversity there are always glimmers of light and Durban was to thrill to the story of one of the most exciting stories of escape from Tobruk, involving three soldiers of the Durban Light Infantry. They were Sergeant A.H. 'Tubby' Goldman, Corporal C.H. Spear and Private V.D. Borain, who shot their way out of the beleaguered fort carrying the regimental colours. Armed with a Bren gun each, with food, but little water, they headed across the desert until, almost collapsing from thirst, and reduced to licking the dew of a derelict truck, Goldman found two 4-gallon drums of water in a dug-out. This unquestionably saved their lives. Unable to carry much of it they were, nevertheless, able to continue their trek for a further four days, resting by day and walking by night, all their waking moments punctuated by hair-raising encounters with German tanks, dispatch-riders, and enemy convoys. On the fifth day, hidden in a derelict German vehicle, a German tank drew up a mere 50 yards distant and within minutes the RDLI men had leapt from their hiding place and shot two of the German tank crew dead and wounded a third. The fourth German, now a prisoner, was made to drive the tank to what they hoped would be the safety of the Allied lines, but it ran out of petrol and had to be abandoned. They left it burning. Eight miles of walking brought them to a bir, a large dried-up underground water storage area, and here they hid, enduring agonizing moments when seven German tanks and two trucks arrived to inspect the bir in search of water. Scarcely breathing and with a revolver dug into the ribs of the captured German with them the South Africans remained in the darkness of the bir until the Germans left. Then their long trek continued – they released their German prisoner because of the total lack of food and water – and at seven o'clock the following morning, desperation now the motivating force, they stopped a German supply truck they saw approaching. In the ensuing fight Goldman shot and killed one German in the truck, accepted the surrender of the other, and then, in the undreamed of luxury of a fully-stocked truck, plentifully supplied with petrol, they drove to the Eighth Army lines, some 300 miles distant, ignoring the attempts that were made to shell them. Goldman was subsequently awarded the DCM.

Another anecdote reached me at about this time and it had a strictly personal appeal. My husband Jack was foraging around Sidi Rezegh after the tide of battle had receded and came upon a cognac bottle boldly labelled in gold letters 'Perla'. He gently eased the label off and sent it to me as a souvenir, not disguising, however, his and his friends' disgust, that the bottle when they found it was empty.

On New Year's Eve, 1942, the *Highland Monarch*, followed by the *Empire Trooper*, sailed into Durban harbour, bringing with them the troops of the 1st South African Division for retraining and regrouping. The strictest security measures about the movement of convoys were still in force, but there was no keeping secret from Durban the fact that the South Africans were coming home. I, deeply security conscious, was horrifed to learn that in Durban receptions for the troops were being planned and that there were even discussions about a triumphal march past. I wrote a letter of protest to a newspaper in which I said:

> 'The fight still goes on, and with tragic reminders at our very door, necessitating the strictest observance of black-outs and "Don't talk about ships" injunctions, are we not courting disaster by making public preparations involving the disclosure of departure and arrival dates of ships?
>
> 'The earliest possible return to his home circle is the all-absorbing wish of every war-weary, battle-scarred hero and my desire to ensure the safe return of our men – including my husband and two sons – is, I am sure, shared by every South African. May I suggest that sober gratitude and safety first, rather than a flag-waving welcome be the wisest course for Durban and Cape Town to steer at this moment.'

My views were supported by an editorial in one of the Durban newspapers which wrote:

> 'Enemy submarines are operating very close to our shores and to advertise the fact that troop transports are within a few hundred miles is surely to invite tragedy. Is it not possible to organize civic receptions

without letting every Tom, Dick and Jane know days beforehand that thousands of South African troops are in the submarine danger zone?'

The warnings had a salutary effect, for, from then on, civic receptions and other welcoming functions were not even talked about until the troops had landed safely. For all this, the reception accorded the returning 1st South African Division was a memorable one. The ships were berthed next to each other and the men kept singing ceaselessly with me, but constantly breaking off to break into 'For She's a Jolly Good Fellow'.

By this time my position had been officially formalized. I had been granted a special permit which described me as a 'Dockside Entertainer' – a title which, I understand, was the only one of its kind issued by the Allied authorities anywhere in the world. While this permit gave me considerable freedom of movement in the docks, and while, of course, I had by now become a familiar figure to all the officers – naval and military – stationed at the docks, I went to great pains never to abuse the unique position I held. I never once went aboard any of the ships – not even the hospital ships, which were exempt from many of the more rigid security precautions. Once, at the height of the war I had a call from a Durban newspaper asking if there were any truth in the rumour that my dockside entertainer's permit had been withdrawn from me following a complaint by an admiral. I was told that a British admiral had said that he could hear me singing 6 miles out to sea, and that, if the Navy could hear my voice, then so could the enemy. Six miles! My singing master, Stephen Mavrogodarto, would have regarded that as a compliment to his training.

That I was known, virtually throughout the free world, as 'The Lady in White' I learned at five o'clock one morning in

1942. I had gone to the docks, as usual, to sing, when a customs officer stopped to show me a copy of *The Flying Dutchman*, the ship's magazine of the troopship *Westernland*. Dated 18 June 1942, it had this article in it:

'We had a pretty good time in Durban – the camp was easy, the town was hospitality itself, and the food was cheap, excellent and abundant. We didn't hang the flags out when the time came for leaving. As usual, we were up on that fateful day at some godless hour of the morning and after the usual hanging around, reached the ship about 11 o'clock.

'We stowed our kit on board and gathered on the rails to see the last of the town. There was not much to see, only the normal dockside litter of cranes, sheds, rails, trucks, ropes and so forth, with a few civilians waving good-bye beyond the dock gates.

'We were all "cheesed" in varying degrees.

'Cars came and went, driven by immaculate Waafs and depositing or whisking away still more immaculate dock-side officers and officials. Only one car stayed – a black sedan driven by a woman dressed in white, wearing a big red straw hat.

'No one took much notice of her as she threaded her way towards us round the piles of wood and ropes, and over railway lines and under steel hawsers. She was not remarkable in any way, being of an age when a year or so either way doesn't matter much. She had pleasant features and was of a build that the French describe as *en bon point*. Then she started to sing.

She had come down to the docks to give the boys a last song. To the most unmusical ear it was obvious that she possessed a voice of no mean quality, a rich soprano that could beat low, deep and vibrant, or trill, pure and flutelike on the high notes.

'She sang for *hours* all the songs we knew. Songs we'd learned as kids and are known wherever the English language is spoken. Songs we'd heard way back home, at the cinema, the theatre, over the radio or in the dance hall. Popular tunes we'd sung at camp concerts, or ship sing-songs, and songs one usually heard in concert halls with spotlight and piano accompaniment.

'Yet they lost nothing, rather did they gain in meaning and eloquence coming from this lone white figure picking her way to and fro along the dingy quayside.

'As she sang, she held her audience enthralled. No longer was it a roar of approval as a well-known tune was caught up and hurled back by a thousand throats – but a queerer feeling held and gripped me.

'A strange contraction of the throat – a deeper appreciation of those words caught us and conjured up before our eyes other scenes, maybe another woman – many thousands of miles away. The chorus started, wavered, and fell away to poignant silence.

'Gradually we drew away from the quayside, but still the lilting words pursued us. At the end of the jetty that white-clad singer started to sing "Auld Lang Syne" and as the gap grew between ship and the shore only snatches of the song were wafted to us on the breeze. Finally, just a picture of that solitary figure waving a red hat high above her head – yet we swear she was still singing.

'So we left Durban, city of a thousand pleasant memories. Yet when many of these are forgotten or are but dimly seen through the mist of passing years, one memory will stand out bright and clear, and many a mind will recall with feelings of pleasure the songs of the 'LADY IN WHITE'.

5

'Paraphernalia for the use of'

In the first months of the war I had some difficulty with what, in military jargon, would I suppose fall under the heading 'Dockside Entertainer: Paraphernalia for the use of'.

Initially I used to sing through cupped hands if there was a high wind blowing, but this wasn't particularly satisfactory and I was delighted when, one blustering morning, as I was singing to a departing convoy, Jean Marie, our family chauffeur, handed me a small celluloid megaphone. My father had sent it down to the docks to me. I was not to have it for long, though. It 'joined' the 6th Grenadier Guards on a day that was memorable for the Guards as well as for me.

The ships were lined up at the quayside awaiting the troops that would board them and soon through the dock gates swung the leading units of the 6th Grenadier Guards, their iron shod boots beating a tattoo on the concrete paving. Smartly, they marched to the quayside and were brought to a stop in front of a small, scruffy-looking ship, so low in the water it was possible almost to step aboard her from the quayside. The impact on the Guards could be felt rather than seen, although in the sternly disciplined faces of some of the officers I did detect a look that was a mixture of disbelief and aristocratic disdain. It was easy to sense their thoughts – 'This tub for the Guards! . . .'

They went aboard and the atmosphere was icy as I stood alongside the ship and began to sing 'The British Grenadiers'. There was no response at first. Their pre-occupation with their ship-board accommodation was all-embracing, but doggedly I sang on and finally began to sense a thawing in their attitude. They listened intently, then first one voice and then another took up the refrain and soon they were all singing. I was struck particularly by a powerful and melodious voice belonging to a young Guardsman and soon he and I were doing a duet together to the delight of the other Guardsmen, who by now seemed to have forgotten their disgruntlement. As the ship started its preparations to pull away the atmosphere was vastly changed, but I realized it wouldn't be long before the discomfort of their surroundings would again come uppermost in their minds. So I handed my little megaphone to the young singer and urged him to carry on singing to keep up the spirits of his comrades and to continue singing with me until they were out of hearing.

The final chapter to this story was told to me some years later by the officer commanding the battalion, Brigadier Archer Clive, who returned to Durban later in the war to take up a military liaison post. Many of those Guardsmen, he told me, had died storming the Mareth Line, among them John, the singer. There was a further sequel – one of those strange coincidences which were to occur with such surprising frequency in my life. I was in Manchester in 1960 driving in a taxi to the annual banquet of the British Legion there. I struck up a conversation with the driver and it transpired that he was among those on board the scruffy little ship and that he, too, had been wounded in the Mareth Line while serving as batman to Brigadier Archer Clive.

Another equally odd coincidence occurred in 1963 when I was outside Buckingham Palace and a London 'Bobby' came up to me. He had been aboard the 'scruffy' little ship on that day in Durban and remembered vividly the incident of the celluloid megaphone. We reminisced briefly and then he warmly shook my hand, saying 'Let me thank you now for what you did then'.

I had gone back to cupped hands once the guards had sailed, but relief was not long in coming – and from a totally unexpected source. The *Llandaff Castle* – a very old 'friend', to which I had sung on so many occasions – was torpedoed and sunk only a day's sailing from Durban – and safety. The survivors were being brought to Durban and our dockside canteen geared itself to cope with this emergency. All through the night of 3 December 1942 – it was pouring with rain – we waited until in the grey, moist dawn, we saw the silhouette of HMS *Inconstant* coming into dock, her decks crowded with bedraggled survivors wearing all sorts of odd scraps of clothing. Anything but downcast, as we expected them to be, they shouted, the moment they saw me, 'Give us a song', and I responded with 'There'll Always Be an England'. Lustily they joined in and as the song ended they gave a great burst of cheering before trooping down the gangways to be fed and clothed.

A moving reunion took place in Durban in the course of this *Llandaff Castle* episode. On board the sinking ship were Mr and Mrs G. Gleadell and their three children aged 4 and 2 years and 3 months. When the first torpedo struck, Mrs Gleadell took one child, her husband another and a steward grabbed the baby. When they reached the deck the steward with the baby was nowhere to be seen, so Mr Gleadell, after pushing his wife and two children into a lifeboat, went below deck in search of their baby.

In the night, Mrs Gleadell, her two children huddled close to her, heard a baby crying – in another lifeboat. Frantically she shouted and the two lifeboats came alongside each other and Mrs Gleadell was reunited with her baby. But her husband was missing. Five days later, in Durban, Mrs Gleadell was reunited with her husband, whom she had given up as lost. He had stayed in the *Llandaff Castle* frantically searching until the end and then had scrambled into a life-boat to be picked up and brought into Durban after his wife and family had already been safely landed.

HMS *Inconstant* had been in Durban for a few days when Seaman Charles Yarnell came to see me at the dockside canteen and presented me with a strong black vulcanite megaphone with a card on which was written 'With grateful thanks from the survivors of the *Llandaff Castle*'. That megaphone remained my constant companion. When not in use it was always in the back of my car in case it should ever be needed. One night my car was stolen and eventually recovered by the police in Johannesburg – 400 miles away – but the megaphone had gone.

My third, and remaining megaphone, was presented to me after the war had ended in circumstances which will remain always a sentimental reminder of my long association with the Royal Navy. HMS *Nigeria*, with Admiral Sir Desmond McCarthy, CB, DSO, Commander-in-Chief South Atlantic on board sailed into Durban in July 1950 for his farewell visit. In accordance with my undertaking to keep on singing, even in peacetime, to ships of the Royal Navy whenever they put into Durban, I was at the docks and received an invitation to come aboard the flagship. Escorted up the gangway by Captain Scott, I was presented with the most magnificent burnished copper megaphone, on which was a brass shield surmounted with the crest of the Royal Navy and with the following inscription:

'To the Lady in White from HMS Nigeria. 10.7.50.'

In making the presentation Captain Scott said to me: 'This is not only from the men of HMS *Nigeria*, but from all men of the British Navy to thank you for what you did for their morale during the war.'

Determined never to lose this megaphone, I agreed to the request made by the Durban branch of the MOTHS

(Memorable Order of Tin Hats) that it be lodged, as one of the mementoes of my wartime career, with their branch HQ. I use it now only on very special occasions.

Hats were another part of my 'Paraphernalia for the use of'. At first I used to wear an old panama hat that matched the rest of my uniform, but on those scorching days in the open dock area it didn't give anything like the shade needed. So I bought a large straw hat that could, more accurately, be described as a small sunshade. While this was effective in the sun, it leaked like a sieve whenever it rained. I resuscitated my old white panama and instructed our gardener to give it a couple of good coatings of red duco paint. It worked like a charm. I had a glamorous, almost indestructible, hat for the hot summer days – and one off which the water simply cascaded whenever it rained.

It came in useful when an emergency arose on the day the hospital ship *Atlantis* was being loaded with patients brought from the military hospital in Johannesburg and now bound for England. The sun was beating down mercilessly as the stretcher-bearers hurried between the ship and trains, alongside which I had taken up position to renew acquaintance with the men to whom I had sung when they had first been brought to South Africa as patients. Lying on a stretcher on the hot asphalt, a man was obviously in great distress. While awaiting for orderlies to arrive and shift him, I sheltered him from the burning sun with my faithful red sombrero.

Right from the beginning of my dockside career I had to make adjustments to my singing technique to ensure my voice would carry sufficiently far across the water, and then, as a ship drew alongside, would bridge the very much narrower gap. For long distance singing it would be pitched in a higher register, which sometimes left me in no end of difficulty with the top notes. Then, singing close to a ship's side I had to look upwards, which not only gave me a crick in the neck but tended to contract the throat muscles. Whatever conditions had to be overcome the teachings of my singing master, Stephen Mavrogodarto – open throat with no extraneous muscle tension – were borne in mind. But for his training, I would never have been able to keep going day in and day out for all the years that I did.

— 6 —

The Royal Navy

Durban in wartime was a vital strategic link in Britain's chain of overseas bases, so, not surprisingly, the ships of the Royal Navy were frequent visitors. Indeed, I do not think a day went past when from my window at Pineholme I was not able to see the dawn silhouettes of mighty battleships and the businesslike shapes of cruisers and destroyers as they lay in the harbour. Many of them bore names that are among the most glorious in British naval tradition – *Nelson, Valiant, Resolution, Queen Elizabeth, Warspite, Barham, Royal Sovereign, Revenge, Renown, Repulse* and many others – names that are the drum-beats of history. And manning them were the men who were heirs to the heroes who smashed the might of the French fleet at Trafalgar; who humbled, in the First World War, the arrogant German Grand Fleet in the thunderous dawn of Jutland. And now, once again, the Royal Navy was at its battle stations around the world.

Many of the warships spent long spells in Durban undergoing refits. Then there were several based on Durban. So the ships of the Royal Navy and the men aboard them, by reason of the topsyturvy world in which we were living, had a sense of permanence about them and came to be regarded as part – a thrilling and glamorous part – of the local scene. But they were playing a dangerous game in which the stakes were appallingly high, and it was always with a sense of deep personal shock that I learned that this or that ship had gone to the bottom. No fewer than sixteen of the naval ships to which I sang during the war were sunk by the enemy with enormous loss of life.

The first battleship flying the White Ensign to sail into Durban in wartime was the *Royal Sovereign*. It was 22 October 1940, and she limped in to undergo a major refit after a brush with the enemy in the Mediterranean. She presented a majestic sight sailing slowly through the harbour entrance, her crew lining her decks and cheering as I sang their welcome.

In the succeeding months I sang to HMS *Cornwall* and HMS *Dorsetshire*, both to meet their doom from Japanese 'kamikaze' pilots; to HMS *Encounter*,which went down in the battle of the Java Sea, and to the aircraft carrier *Hermes*, which suffered a similar fate. But it was in December 1941 that Durban was to provide the curtain-raiser to Britain's greatest modern naval disaster, one that sent a shudder through every land that was fighting for freedom.

Familiar sights in Durban at that time were HMS *Repulse* and HMS *Prince of Wales*. Only about a month before they sailed on what was to be their last voyage they escorted a convoy to the Middle East, in one of the ships of which was my husband Jack. I therefore had a more than usually deep personal interest in these mighty war vessels and the men in them. The *Prince of Wales*, was, of course, a veteran of the *Bismarck* action, and when she and the *Repulse* received the signal to make for the Far East, the objective was to deter the Japanese from declaring war and to demonstrate the Mother Country's commitment to defend Australia and New Zealand in the event of a Japanese attack.

From Durban they sailed to Singapore and on 2 December they left there for Malaya. It was an assignment that at the time did not hold within it the seeds of disaster, for Japan, was, theoretically anyway, neutral. But unseen submarines were nevertheless shadowing the British ships and the sky would be speckled at times with the dots of reconnaissance aircraft.

Then came 7 December – the 'Day of Infamy' – when Pearl Harbour was attacked without warning. The free world and Japan were at war. For the British task force, forging through the deep green sea, cleft with foaming lines of whiteness where their bows plunged, mortal danger now lay all around. On 10 December the unseen shadows suddenly matierialized and throughout the ships of the task force sounded the alarm 'enemy aircraft approaching'. Seconds later the bombs were falling.

The *Repulse* was struck by a direct hit on its catapult deck and this was followed up by a mass attack by torpedo bombers. Meanwhile, the *Prince of Wales* had fared no better. Her steering gear had gone, and the great ship was out of control. Soon, her sides ripped open by torpedoes, the *Repulse* began sinking, and almost simultaneously, the *Prince of Wales* keeled over and disappeared beneath the waves. In a single stroke the Japanese had destroyed all effective opposition in the South China Sea and the Indian Ocean. The news reached us in Durban with the impact of deep personal loss, for no fewer than 47 officers and 793 men died in that double tragedy – men whom we in Durban had known as friends.

The *Barham* was another battleship familiar to wartime Durbanites. It came in first in June 1941 for repairs to a gaping hole in its bows, and among the members of its crew who became frequent visitors to Pineholme was Ronald Kennedy, of St. Andrews, Fife, the only son of Colonel Kennedy of the Scots Guards. Ronald Kennedy had won the Silver Dirk as the best cadet at Dartmouth and we naturally followed his career with close interest. He sailed from Durban in the *Barham* and when this great ship was torpedoed off Sollum and sunk within minutes, we grieved for the great loss of life that accompanied this naval disaster but believed that Ronald was safe, as he had told us before leaving that he was expecting to be transferred from the

Barham to another ship. A few days later, however, we received a letter from Lt Robert Barlow, of the minelayer *Latona*, telling us that Ronald had been transferred from the *Barham* and had joined the *Latona*, only to be killed when it was attacked by enemy aircraft.

I remained in close touch with Ronald's parents, who came to look upon me as the only remaining close link with the son they were never to see again. After the war my daughter and I paid a visit to them in St. Andrews in Scotland.

The aircraft carrier HMS *Illustrious* held a special place in my affections, for it was a case of love at first sight. I was to sing many times to the crew lining the decks of that mighty ship as she came into and sailed from Durban, and in due course I received a letter from John Whitehouse, editor of the ship's magazine *The Beacon*. It reads:

'Dear Madam Perla,

'Someone mentioned in my hearing this morning, "I hope that lady is there this morning" – and I felt sure you would be and told him so.

'You were! We were all delighted and dipped our Ensign to you and, more than that, sounded the "Attention" with every man standing to attention in salute of a grand job of work – in salute to you. A fragment of time, in silence, because words fail to thank you as you deserve to be thanked.

'Had you not been there a legend would have been shattered and I ask you always to continue this – for the sake of those who have heard of you, and who, in passing, desire to participate in the story and to say you have tuned your lay specially for them too.

'Thank you for every kindness and thank you, too, for all the other chaps who might not have known just how to say it or who never had a chance to.'

On one occasion there was a joyous lunch-time concert in the docks, with the crew of *Illustrious* joining in the choruses and then singing specially for me 'Just an Old Fashioned Lady'. The following day the ship sailed for some unknown destination, that would, I imagined, keep her at sea for weeks, possibly months. My surprise was easily understandable when a few days later I saw her passing through the harbour entrance, and as it drew closer to the North Pier I raised my megaphone and sang 'Here We Are Again'. There was a great burst of laughter from the crew of 2,000. In accordance with my habit of never prying into security affairs, I never did discover the reason for the sudden return.

The special request on that day was for 'Happy Birthday' and I learned it was for a seaman named Eric Smith, who was celebrating his 19th birthday on board. I slipped into town and returned with an iced birthday cake, which I sent aboard addressed to Eric Smith, only to be told that there were no fewer than 325 Smiths on board. Nothing fazed, the officer to whom I handed the cake assured me that the correct Smith would be found. He was. I received a grateful letter of thanks from him.

HMS *Ramillies* had a special liking for that old drinking song 'Sweet Nellie Dean', which I sang with great gusto to her crew as she sailed from Durban on 10 September 1943, and received later a message from Commander Behan thanking me for my singing and saying what a morale-lifting effect it had had on his crew.

When HMS *Elizabeth* sailed into Durban on 3 October 1944, I, at my usual post, had just ended singing a welcome when a man's voice, loud and clear, came echoing across the water from the ship. It was the ship's commander, who, through a loud-hailer, said, 'Thank you, Perla. It's very good of you to come down and welcome us so early in the morning.' Later Captain H.G. Norman, of HMS *Elizabeth*, invited me to come aboard, but conscious always of adhering strictly to the conditions of my 'Dockside Entertainer's' pass, I declined with thanks, adding 'Not until they sound the last all clear'.

HMS *Ceylon* had a dual reason for imprinting itself on my memory. Her chaplain, the Rev. Colin Stephenson was one of the most handsome men I have ever seen in my life and had the further merit of possessing a great love of singing. He organized a small choir on board, and when HMS *Ceylon* was in harbour he brought them to Pineholme, their voices joining mine in an evening of singing. Among those in the choir whom I remember particularly were Lt. David Biddulph, ERA C. Motton, AB W.A. Berner, ERA A. Jackson and AB Michael Dove, Harry Clarke, and W.J. Ellis.

Colin Stephenson was later to suffer serious injury in a way totally unconnected with the sea. He was collecting plants in Ceylon and fell from a tree into a disused well. The story could easily have had a tragic ending but for the fact that an Indian girl saw the incident and went for help. Both his legs were broken and one was eventually amputated below the knee, but his spirit remained undaunted and when I next saw him he was Vicar at St. Mary Magdalen at Oxford. I sang at a parish Christmas party that he organized. He is now Master of the Anglican priory at Walsingham, and when I went to visit him there he expressed his delight at our reunion in these words, written in my autograph book:

> 'From Bloemfontein's zenanas,
> To far Kaffraria kraals,
> Where hosts of ripe bananas,
> Blow down in tropic squalls
> The men who came to Durban

Were met by glorious sight
For there upon the quayside
A Lady all in white.
What though the spicy breezes
Blow soft o'er Zanzibar,
Where everyone one sees is
As black as streams of tar.
For when we came to Durban
We heard the sailors choice,
As through the "Ceylon's" portholes
There floated Perla's voice.'

'Operation Ironclad' – the code name for the invasion of Madagascar, provided the greatest concentration of British Naval might that Durban had seen, or was to see, in World War II. On 22 April 1942, there was assembled in the harbour an armada that included the battleship *Ramillies*, the aircraft carrier *Illustrious*, 2 cruisers, 11 destroyers, a flotilla of minesweepers and corvettes, plus 13 assault ships, as well as all the transport that were to carry the invading forces. Excitement in Durban ran high and speculation was rife as to the destination of this huge and powerful force. One Durban matron whispered confidentially to me that she had it 'on the highest authority' that it was bound for the Mediterranean to invade neutral Turkey. Others were certain that some spectacular form of direct help to the hard-pressed Russians lay behind the plan. No one even guessed that Madagascar, held by Vichy France, was the objective. The secrecy which was maintained was remarkable and was to earn a warm tribute from Sir Winston Churchill, who, after the war, wrote: 'The Madagascar episode was in its secrecy of planning and precision of tactical execution a model of amphibious descents.'

In command of the huge naval force was a South African, Rear-Admiral E.N. Syfret, who was born in Cape Town and joined the Royal Navy in 1904. The land forces were commanded by Major-General E.G. Sturgess, of the Royal Marines. I was at my place on the North Pier on 28 April when the great force sailed out of the harbour, and, as I sung to each ship as it passed, I was saluted in return. A week later the task force, fortified by the addition of HMS *Indomitable*, was within striking distance of the objective, the main harbour of Madagascar, and a few days later the flag of Vichy France had been struck and replaced by the Union Jack. The invasion resulted in only 400 Allied army casualties and the victory, won at a time when Britain was sorely in need of success, sent a thrill through the free world. Some two months were to elapse before the whole island was occupied, but the importance of 'Ironclad' lay in the fact that it represented the first amphibious operation since the Dardanelles, twenty-seven years earlier, in World War I.

As was the case with most naval ships, there were always certain members of the crews whom I came to know particularly well by reason of their ships being frequent visitors to Durban. Alfred Taylor, of HMS *Valiant*, was an old friend of mine who was often a guest at Pineholme where he delighted us with his 'Pop-eye the Sailor Man' imitations. With him was Dan O'Regan, another friend. He and Taylor later served in HMS *Phoebe*, and, in action off Tobruk, O'Regan was awarded the DCM, only, however, to forfeit his life some months later when he was serving aboard HMS *Neptune* when it was blown up in an Italian minefield. Other members of the *Valiant*'s crew who knew Pineholme well were Signalman Leslie Philips, of Durham, Jack Harding, of Coventry, and Jack Farmer.

One of the lighter moments of the fleet's stay in Durban was provided by the crew of HMS *Revenge*, commanded by

Captain Llewellyn V. Morgan. They gave a concert in the Durban City Hall entitled 'Round the Bend' and received a rousing reception from a packed hall.

HMS *Renown*, escorted by four destroyers, made a majestic entrance into Durban just before Christmas 1944, and, though I was on the North Pier singing with all my might, it was, I felt, a losing battle. A raging wind was blowing that made it difficult to even keep my feet. I was told later, however, by men on board the *Renown* that they had heard me above the howling wind. The battleship spent some time in Durban and several of her crew were guests at Pineholme. One of them, Midshipman David Mudford, was to give me a vivid reminder of how long the war had now lasted. He brought me greetings from his father, Captain J.F.W. Mudford, of HMS *Frobisher*, to which I had sung years before in the war when she had come into Durban. At that time the young, fresh-faced midshipman from the Renown must still have been a schoolboy. Two other midshipmen came with Mudford. They were Derek Sanders and Desmond Grundy.

HMS *Renown* remained in Durban for so long a period that it became possible for me to organize lunch-time singing concerts for the crews and it was at one of these that I met Captain Brooke, in command of the *Renown*, who told me how deeply the Navy appreciated my singing and, more important, the fact that I never once let down the men who, knowing Durban was their destination, would ask sometimes with voices that would quiver slightly at the thought of possible disappointment, whether I would be there to welcome them. Captain Brooke was something of a rarity among naval officers. Instead of transferring from ship to ship as so many of them did, Captain Brooke started as midshipman on board HMS *Renown* when she was being built and ended up being her captain. He had developed, he told me, such a strong possessive sense about the mighty battleship that he felt he would like to suggest to the Lords of the Admiralty that when the ship, like himself, had ended a lifetime of usefulness to her country, she should be allowed to spend her remaining years with him in his garden.

HMS *Renown*'s bosun was David Ford, who can add to his wartime achievements a record that I doubt will ever be equalled. For a bet he clambered 65 ft. up to the top of a wharfside crane and then dived into the sea over two submarines that were lying alongside each other, moored to the quay. The bosun won his bet, but history does not record what disciplinary price his naval officers exacted from him for his dangerous exploit.

The sailing of HMS *Renown* on 26 February 1945 was the severing of a bond of close friendship and it was an emotional moment for me as I stood listening to the Royal Marine Band, lined up on the *Renown*'s deck, playing under the baton of Mr Leslie 'I'll See You Again'. I responded with 'Land of Hope and Glory' and 'Rule Britannia' and then, as the ship drew further away from the quay, Captain Brooke's voice rang out across the water, 'Goodbye, Perla, and thank you very much'.

When HMS *Battler*, an aircraft carrier, was in Durban in 1944, I was to be paid what I regard as one of the most glowing compliments of all time. It reached me through a letter from AB Ian Overall, who said, in words that practically breathed his own incomprehension, 'It may sound incredible, but when it was piped around the ship that the Lady in White was on the jetty a host of the chaps actually left the dinner queue to hear you sing. That was some sacrifice, because it's always a fight to keep one's place in the queue at the best of times.'

HMS *Battler* was accompanied on her visit to Durban in 1944 by another aircraft carrier, HMS *Unicorn*, which, with

1944: Singing to *HMS Battler*, one of the Navy's latest aircraft carriers. But –

Greetings from
Gerta Seidli Ósoron

– 'turn round', must have said the photographer, 'and let the camera see who's singing!'

four other carriers, were brought from the United States under the command of Captain C.D. Yates, whom I was to meet more than a year after my victory over the HMS *Battler* 'gastronomes'. Captain Yates was in hospital in Durban, recovering from having been gassed when putting up a smoke screen in the Mediterranean.

The crew of HMS *Battler* was among the most enthusiastic audiences I ever sang to in the war. After hearing me on the morning of their arrival, they asked me to come back that evening – which I did – and after that we held regular dockside concerts. Before *Battler* sailed Captain F.W. Stephenson wrote in my autograph book: 'To the Lady in White whom all officers and ratings in my ship will remember as one of the greatest tonics of the war.'

When the *Battler* was about to sail we had a great farewell singsong on the dockside, in the course of which the ship's photographer came ashore to photograph me with the *Battler* in the background. I was later to learn, from the same letter in which Ian Overall had told me about the men deserting the chow queue, that the entire ship's company queued up to buy copies of the photograph. I received my copy in due course and one of them was published in the London *Sketch* in 1950 as an illustration for the 'Candid Cameo' written by Noel Langley. It prompted Captain Stephenson, living in retirement, to write to say how proud he and his former shipmates were that it was their ship, the *Battler*, which featured in the *Sketch* article about me.

The *Sketch* article in question had an interesting background. Lady Joy Packer, wife of Admiral Sir Herbert Packer, who was in command of HMS *Warspite* at one time in the war, and who later spent several years in command of the Simonstown Naval Base, introduced me to Captain J.E. Broome (Ret.), the editor of the *Sketch*. Being a former naval officer, he was most interested in my wartime singing career, and decided to invite Noel Langley to contribute a candid cameo of me. At the same time he asked me to write a 200-word 'reply' to Noel Langley's contribution to be published at the same time. But I declined and submitted instead these few lines:

> 'I sang a song into the air
> And the song from beginning to end
> I found again in the heart of a friend.'

Lady Packer, who is the author of many successful books, mentioned in one of them, *The Grey Mistress*, that I had sung both to her husband and to her son in the course of the war. I have, in fact, a treasured tangible memento of the occasion when I sang to HMS *Warspite* when it was commanded by Admiral Sir Herbert Packer. In 1943 she was in Durban and, having sung a farewell to her, I received in due course a photograph of the Admiral standing alongside his ship, with this inscription:

> 'To the Lady in White from Bertie Packer with many thanks for our send-off in 1943.'

Some years later, in London, I met Sir Herbert, who expressed his delight at having a close-up look at me. 'Previously I have only been able to see you through my binoculars from the bridge of the *Warspite*.'

Having, in the war, seen almost the entire might of Britain's Navy, it came as something of a surprise to be introduced to the greatest battleship of them all, HMS *Howe*, just as the final curtain was falling on the tragedy that had lasted for almost five long years. Only a few weeks before the atom bombs were to be dropped on Japan to bring hostilities to a precipitate end, the 45,000-ton HMS *Howe* steamed through Durban's harbour entrance. I was there to greet her. She remained in Durban during those historic days that saw the devastating birth of the atomic era and on VJ Day the captain and officers gave a party in the Durban Club to celebrate the advent of peace throughout the world.

An invitation was sent to me, delivered personally by one of HMS *Howe*'s marines, Corporal Cyril Kingham, who was of such striking appearance that I painted his portrait in oils with a map of the world as a backdrop, indicative of the many theatres of the world in which he had seen active service.

The mighty guns of HMS *Howe* were painted in bright red-lead and this made such a striking and colourful contrast with the overall greyness that I was compelled to capture in oils the exciting picture she presented. The painting was subsequently on view at an exhibition held by the Victoria League in London, where it caught the attention of Earl Howe (Lord Curzon). He bought it and it hangs today in his ancestral home at Penn, in Buckinghamshire. It was, he told me, the only painting he had ever seen of the battleship that bore the name of his famed naval ancestor.

When HMS *Howe* sailed from Durban on 10 September there was a big crowd to see her off. For me it was a notable occasion for one particular reason. Having sung, day in and day out for all the war years without any accompaniment, I was, on this occasion, to find that the Royal Marine bandmaster had assembled the ship's band on deck and had planned a programme specially for me to sing to. As the great ship began its preparations for casting off the bandmaster raised his baton, glanced over his shoulder at me and then, with a precision that belonged to the concert hall, the orchestral strains of 'There'll Always Be an England' were blended with my voice, and a hush fell over the crowd. 'Wish Me Luck as You Wave Me Goodbye;' followed and then 'Land of Hope and Glory' and 'Rule

Britannia'. The great ship drew slowly away and as I sang there stirred through me a sense of inexpressible gratitude that the world was once more indeed at peace.

It was rare for me to sing in French, but an opportunity to do so occurred in 1945 when the battleship *Richelieu* came into Durban and was berthed not far from HMS *Howe*. There was a great deal of friendly bantering as to which of the two ships was the bigger with, as far as I can remember, the French ship being the winner by being a mere 18 inches longer than her British counterpart. She was due to sail at dawn on 10 August, and before the first rays of the rising sun had begun to gild the rooftops of Durban, I was huddled beneath a dim light in the docks swotting the words of 'J'attendrai'. Then, from my usual place on the North Pier, I waited until the ship, heading for the harbour mouth, drew opposite me. I began to sing. The crew were lined up like ramrods on the deck – the perfect picture of a well-disciplined ship leaving harbour. Being thus unable to give vent to normal Gallic exuberance was apparently too much for one of the sailors who, I noticed delightedly, gave a surreptitious little wave of his hand to me from knee level. It was a charming, heart-warming gesture.

Durban's own warship HMSAS *Natal*, under the command of Lt. Commander D.A. Hall, DSO, returned home on what was an unfortunately timed occasion. It was July Handicap Day, with practically the entire city, if not at the race-course, then totally preoccupied with what is South Africa's greatest annual event in the racing calendar. *Natal* was arriving virtually unnoticed as a result – a fate which she certainly did not deserve for she has to her eternal renown the historic achievement of sinking a German submarine – the U 766 – when on her maiden voyage from the shipbuilding yards at Newcastle-upon-Tyne.

I sang a welcome to HMSAS *Natal* on this July Handicap

Day and received in return a wonderful photograph of her entering Durban harbour, with the Bluff in the background and showing the crew, their arms raised and caps in hand, giving three cheers for me. The inscription read: 'Thank you for giving us such a wonderful welcome. From the Officers and men of HMSAS Natal.' It was signed by Lt. Commander Hall.

The South African ship numbered among her crew some coloured sailors, and as the ship was being tied up alongside the quay I asked them if they had any specially favoured songs they would like to hear. To my surprise they asked for 'There'll Always Be an England', and on my pressing them for the reason, one of them said, 'You see lady, if it were not for England we wouldn't have a ship like this'.

There was no sentiment with which I was in more whole-hearted agreement and I sang the song they asked for.

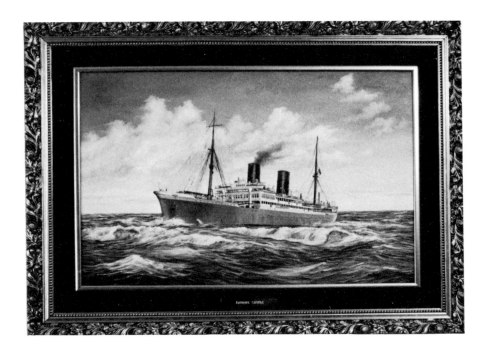

Arundel Castle, 19,216 tons. Built 1921. Sister ship to *Windsor Castle* (sunk by enemy March 1943). [The Castle-'boats' sailed over 7,000,000 miles during World War Two – the *Arundel Castle* alone clocking half-a-million of them. Fourteen were lost through enemy action.]

In May Ivor L. Lea of Thornton Cleveleys, Lancs. wrote to *Saga* magazine: 'I spent many years on Union Castle ships, particularly *Arundel Castle*. I well remember Mrs Gibson who, in fair weather or foul, stood on the bluff point at Durban and sang to all troopships. Her favorite song was 'Land of Hope and Glory' and this would sound fantastic as we sailed up the bay to our allotted berth in Durban harbour.

I deeply regret the passing of so many of our wonderful merchant ships. Please find enclosed a photograph of my painting of the old *Arundel*. I loved every rivet of her!'

In January 1991, I wrote to ask for a photograph of his painting for possible inclusion in this book, only to learn from his wife that he had died three months earlier. But with her letter she enclosed a beautiful colour photograph of her husband's painting – here presented in half-tone – a fitting tribute to a gallant man and a gallant ship. (Ed.)

7

The unsung heroes

But peace was only a yearned-for – almost a forlorn – hope in those months early in the war when the free world was reeling under the enormous losses being inflicted on Britain's Merchant Navy. Winston Churchill, in those dark days, paid a glowing tribute in the House of Commons to those unsung heroes – the merchant seamen. 'Nothing daunts the ardour of the Merchant Navy,' he said, 'their toils and tireless courage are our salvation. The sea traffic upon which we, as a nation, depend for our very existence proceeds without interrruption.'

How fervently I echoed those sonorous phrases, for to me the Merchant Navy typified all that is great in the British character. The merchant ships, many of them old and grimy, with living conditions on board devoid almost of basic comfort, came and went through all the war years, carrying out their tasks with none of the glamour that always surrounded the Royal Navy. How more fittingly, I always felt, the appellation 'The Silent Service' applied to the merchant navy rather than to the fighting arm.

During the war years the staggering total of 45,000 ships called at South Africa's ports. There were 400 convoys, with a total of 6,000,000 men, and more than half these ships passed through Durban. I felt I owed them a special duty for, with the number of sinkings mounting monthly to appalling heights there was no knowing from one day to another which ship would be next to feel the sickening thud of a torpedo smashing into her sides. From those simple, good-natured sailors, leaning eagerly over the side, many of them in pants and vests covered in oil and grime, I received always the most heartfelt gratitude for the songs I sang to them.

Except for the Queens – *Elizabeth* and *Mary* – Durban saw in the war all the greatest liners afloat, among them the *Ile de France*, the *Mauretania* and the *Nieuw Amsterdam*. They were regular callers – operating a shuttle service. The most spectacular assembly of merchant shipping was in May 1944, when, looking out from my window at Pineholme, the entire harbour area was bristling with tall masts and carved into the horizon were the silhouettes of more than 100 ships, totalling 756,000 tons.

It was, as I have said, a point of great concern to me that the merchant seamen were, so to speak, the backroom boys of the war at sea. There was not even a song dedicated to them and to their stirring achievements, and I made mention of this fact one day at a concert in the Seamen's Institute. My views were published by a columnist in one of Durban's newspapers. The result was astounding. Verses and tunes poured in to the columnist and in due course he selected one which he considered most effectively sang the praises of the men of the 'Fourth' fighting service. The song was written by my father, Otto Siedle, and it was set to music by Mrs. Nan Haverfield, of Durban. It was sung for the first time – by my group of singers and myself – at a concert in the Durban City Hall.

These are the words of it:

1st Verse:
> They sail the seven seas, they bring us what we lack,
> And to our brave 'front liners' they take the foodstuffs back.
> In fo'c'sle and in stokehold, or on the bridge at night,
> Whene'er they meet a raider, they are ready for a fight.

Chorus:
    Now here's to the men of the Mercantile Marine,
    They are heroes one and all,
    However tough may be their lot, they answer to the call.

2nd Verse:
    They don't wear gorgeous uniforms, that matters not a
        cuss,
    Because the Merchant Navy are 'Heroes all' to us
    They're rarely ever heard of, and seldom ever seen,
    But here's 'Good Luck', 'God Bless 'em,' to our Mercantile
        Marine.

After this I made a point of singing this song to the merchant ships as they tied up, calling to them, 'This is specially for you – to thank you for all you are doing'.

The first of the big ships to enter Durban was the *Empress of Britain*, which arrived in October 1940 with the *Empress of Canada*, the *Andes* and the *Strathaird*, bringing women and children evacuees from Egypt and Palestine. They were mostly families of British soldiers serving in the Middle East and they remained in Durban and along the Natal South Coast until the war's end, many of the children growing up in Natal and marrying South Africans.

Eighteen days after the *Empress of Britain* had sailed from Durban, she was torpedoed and sunk off the Irish coast.

The resounding victories which a South African Expeditionary Force was achieving in East Africa were brought vividly home to us at the end of 1941 when the *Empire Pride* sailed into Durban crammed with Italian prisoners of war escorted by soldiers of the Natal Mounted Regiment and the South African Heavy Artillery. The cook of the *Empire Pride* one day approached me as I was standing near a mobile canteen and told me that he had a gift for me – a Lion of Judah ring. I did not want to accept it, urging him to keep it and take it home with him, but he insisted, saying 'To me you are my lucky charm. Every time we have sailed in and out of Durban you have sung to me, so I want you to have this ring as a keepsake. But you must make one promise – you must always sing to us. As long as I hear your voice I know everything is going to be all right.'

I still have that ring. Whenever I look at it I say a little prayer and hope the cook's luck held throughout the war.

Ships bringing Italian prisoners of war were, of course, frequent arrivals, especially in the early stages when the Italian army in East Africa and in the Western Desert was being mopped up in astronomical numbers. When the *Franconia* paid her first visit with prisoners of war on board she was commanded by Captain James Gordon Partridge Bisset, who was to earn, later in the war, the title 'Never-saw-a-sub' Bisset. It happened this way, he was to tell me later in Durban.

The *Franconia*, after depositing her prisoners of war, sailed for Australia, where Captain Bisset found a signal awaiting him instructing him to fly immediately to Miami. He did so and on arrival stepped straight on to the bridge of the *Queen Mary*, which had on board 8,400 American troops – their destination Australia. The liner, which because of its great speed sailed without a convoy, made first for Rio de Janeiro, there to learn that its whereabouts were well known to the Germans, Lord Haw Haw having boasted that it would be sunk as soon as it left port. Halfway across the South Atlantic on its way to Cape Town radio Tokyo broadcast to the world that she had been sunk with all hands, but it was totally untrue. 'Never-saw-a-sub' Bisset never saw a sub on that occasion or on any other of the 66 Atlantic crossings that he made as commander of the *Queen Mary*.

Peace Time. First-class Long Gallery, *Capetown Castle*.

War Time. The same Long Gallery equipped for troops, early in 1940.

Returning from a 1967 visit to England, Perla receives a prize from Captain
Ronald Wright, now Master of the *Capetown Castle*, and recalls their wartime
memories with the following lines:

To his brave Troopship 'Arundel Castle' throughout the War
From the North Pier, as they crossed the Bar,
I sang songs of Welcome and Godspeed
To our men and Allies in a time of need.

In my autograph book Captain Bisset wrote the following:

'J.G.P. Bisset, Captain of the Franconia, 1940–42, When Perla sang to us several times to our great joy and pleasure.'

A memorable visit of the *Franconia* to Durban occurred on 25 July 1945, when she brought the first contingent of the Sixth South African Division back from Italy. There were scenes of great joy and emotion in the dock area, scenes that were to be repeated a few months later in January when she again sailed in bringing 2,000 South African soldiers home. For me the January arrival of the *Franconia* nearly resulted in my proud record of not having missed welcoming a troopship being broken. She was expected at midday on 6 January, but arrived instead at 9am when I was far from my usual place on the North Pier. Seeing her coming in I started running the length of the pier, spurred on by the delighted cheers of the soldiers lining the decks. When I started to sing I thought my lungs would burst from my exertions, but I soon settled down and was able to chalk up on my record only a 'near miss'.

By this time the master of the *Franconia* was Captain Oliver Bateman, who presented me with a photograph of the ship autographed by her officers.

When she sailed I sang a farewell to them and from Captain Bateman I later received this letter:

'On behalf of all the merchant navy personnel in this vessel, I, as their senior officer, would like to express our deep appreciation at hearing the voice of the Lady in White sing our ship away from the quay when there were no troops on board.

This brought it home to one and all of us that you had a soft spot for the Merchant Navy, which we will remember all our lives. With best wishes from myself and all the men serving under me, I remain,
    One of your audience,
    Oliver Bateman.'

We were constantly being given poignant reminders of the terrible toll that enemy submarines and raiders took of the Merchant Navy. Very few weeks went past in the war that did not see survivors of ships that had been sunk being brought into Durban, many of them in terrible physical condition as the result of the ordeal they had gone through. A particularly black period was in October 1940, when a U-boat pack, operating off the west coast of Africa, sunk 103 merchant ships, totalling 443,000 tons. The U-boat menace was later to manifest itself off the shores of South Africa itself as Britain's counter-measures in the Atlantic grew more effective and forced them to turn to more distant areas for their prey. Minefields were laid off Cape Town at one time and in May 1942 five Japanese submarines were known to be lurking in the Moçambique Channel. They sank twenty ships. There was another black period, with a ruthless sequel, from September to December 1942. The *Laconia*, to which I had often sung, was sailing for Britain with 1,800 Italian prisoners of war on board when she was torpedoed by a German submarine, U-boat 156. On realizing that he had torpedoed a ship with nearly 2,000 of his allied nation's soldiers on board, the U-boat captain sent out a series of radio messages appealing for ships in the vicinity to help in the rescue operations and promising them immunity from attack. His, and other U-boats ordered to the area, were engaged in rescuing *Laconia's* survivors, when an American aircraft arrived over the scene, saw the U-boats, and immediately launched a bombing attack on them. The official German reaction was an order from Admiral Doenitz to the German Navy throughout the world: 'All attempts to rescue crews of sunken ships will cease forthwith.'

Two months later on 1 November, the U-boats struck again, this time only 60 miles distant from Durban. The *Mendoza* went down, but there were many survivors and they were brought into Durban. Then on 1 December the *Nova Scotia*, with 700 Italians on board, was sunk in shark-infested waters off Lourenço Marques and for weeks later bodies came floating ashore off the Natal and Zululand coast. We were told that a Portuguese gun-boat which succeeded in picking up 192 survivors had to fight off blood-crazed sharks which were circling the men clinging to pieces of wreckage and to rafts.

Many of the Merchant Navy sailors were extraordinarily young – mere boys – yet before the war ended many of them were to have endured, in the space of a few years, more danger and physical suffering than normally would be crowded into a whole lifetime at sea. George Taylor, of Thurso, Caithness, Scotland, was a typical example. Before he reached his 17th birthday he had been torpedoed three times. A member of the crew of the *Morialta*, he was one of four out of a total of seventy-three men who managed to scramble on to a raft after the ship had been torpedoed. Then, in what was one of the most amazing incidents of the war at sea, the raft was taken in tow by the submarine that had sunk the *Morialta*, and for two and a half days the submarine pulled the raft behind it until, close to Gibraltar, the rope was cast off and the four men reached safety. On their astounding journey they were provided by the submarine with three hot meals a day.

Taylor next found himself at the receiving end of a torpedo when he was in a troop transport in the North

African landing and woke up in a hospital in Liverpool. The third time was in the S.S. *British Chivalry*, which, in February 1944, was sunk by a Japanese submarine. Unlike his earlier experience with a more gallant enemy, the Japanese submarine crew machine-gunned the ship's survivors as they were pulling away in the lifeboats and Taylor was hit in the ankle, knee, arm and chest. The submarine, in due course, submerged and thirty-nine of the survivors, many of them hideously wounded by the machine-gun attack, climbed into a drifting lifeboat. George Taylor, wearing only a lifebelt, was one of the few who survived thirty-eight days in the boat. One man went mad and jumped overboard, another died of his wounds and a third, losing his reason, tried to chop open the water barrels and had to be physically restrained. The wound in Taylor's chest would close up from time to time and swell internally, causing him excruciating pain, until his shipmates, using a razor blade, cut it open again. Daily they prayed for deliverance, but it was not until they were close to the Seychelles Islands that they were picked up by a ship, which, through a fortuitous circumstance – her engines had broken down – had drifted 50 miles off the course she would normally have taken. When Taylor was eventually brought to Durban for hospital treatment he weighed 109 lb. On that nightmare journey of thirty-eight days in the open boat, he had lost 40 lb.

George Taylor was luckier than many. One British merchant ship was sunk not far out of Durban and twenty-eight survivors drifted in a lifeboat for thirty days before being sighted. In that time twenty of the men had died and another four died within hours of arriving in Durban.

Because we had come to accept it as a tragic, but inevitable, process the constant arrival in Durban of survivors of ships sunk by the enemy we established a special 'comforts for survivors' service as part of the functions of the Seamen's Institute. In 1943 alone we dealt with no fewer than 1,572 survivors.

There were, or course, lighter moments. In May 1943, the *Empire Woodlark* came in with a party of thirty-seven merchant seamen on board who had been prisoners of war in Germany, but were exchanged for an equal number of enemy subjects. They were the happiest group of seamen I had seen in a long time and they were, fortunately, in Durban at the time of the announcement that the campaign in North Africa had ended in an overwhelming victory for the Allied forces. I returned home that day from the docks in the middle of a fierce tropical storm, in which deafening claps of thunder mingled with the joyous ringing of the victory bells from St. Pauls Cathedral.

I sang to some of the biggest liners in the world. I also sang to one of the smallest ocean-going craft ever to sail into Durban. It was the *J. van Rensselaar*, a Dutch tug, manned by Hollanders, which had escaped from Tobruk at the time that Rommel's forces were successfully investing the town and port.

While most of the ships attacked at sea never lived to see another day there were many which succeeded in limping back to port. The tanker *Daronia* arrived in port in August 1944, with two enormous holes in her sides – holes large enough for a double-decker bus to pass through. The amazing thing about it was that the only casualty in the encounter that caused these gaping wounds to the ship was a black eye suffered by one of the sailors. The attack occurred when the ship was some 400 miles from Durban, but she managed to limp back to port under her own steam under the protecting eye of a South African Air Force Catalina aircraft, surviving two gales before making port. The *Daronia* had to be practically rebuilt before she was seaworthy again, more than 800 tons of steel being required to fabricate a new side for her.

The transport *Burma* ran aground off Mombasa in August 1944, but she, too, managed to make Durban under her own steam and went promptly into dry-dock. She had 1,500 Italian prisoners on board who were transferred to camps in South Africa. I struck up a warm friendship with three of the *Burma's* gunners, Frank Carter of London, Benjamin Drury, of Pontefract, and Bill Harrop, of Liverpool. They were three such jolly sailors that I did a painting of them which was afterwards raffled in aid of the funds of the Navy League and today hangs in the League's Club.

Some of the bloodiest chapters that were written in the history of World War II stemmed directly from the decision to wage unrestricted U-boat warfare. But those pages, filled as they are with so much tragedy and suffering, are illumined for all eternity by acts of unbelievable heroism and self-sacrifice by men who went about their wartime duties cloaked in the drab, unpretentious anonymity of the Merchant Navy.

It was an honour to sing to them.

— 8 —

Personal tragedy

It was in 1944 that the suffering which I had for so long shared vicariously with all those families throughout the world whose sons and husbands were fated never to return to them touched me personally – deeply and unforgettably. Within the space of ten days I lost my son, Roy, and my mother.

It was in the fighting around Mount Ornita, a 3,000 ft. snow-capped peak in the Mareth Line in Italy, that Roy, as a member of the Black Watch, was mortally wounded. On patrol in search of an enemy position a German hand-grenade was thrown into the midst of where Roy and his men were lying, listening to the enemy's movements and pin-pointing their exact position. His men managed to carry the badly wounded Roy down the mountain-side to their lines but eight hours later he died. His epitaph, as written to me by his Commanding Officer, Lieut.-Col. Brian Madden, was in these words: 'In spite of his wounds his only concern was to inquire about the safety of the rest of the patrol. He was a gallant fellow and we shall not forget him.

'I hope that you will be able to take some comfort from the thought that he played his part as he would have wished to play it and we who fought with him are proud of him as we know you will be.'

I also received other letters, including one from the regimental padre, the Rev. Joseph Grant, now of Grantham-on-Spey in Scotland, giving me details of the difficulties which had to be overcome in bringing the wounded down from the mountain top. Stretcher-bearers were stationed at at distances of 200 yards and the casualties were passed from one to the other, and long and agonizing process.

Roy was buried on the banks of the River Garigliano.

In Durban I had, two weeks earlier, experienced what I now know was a premonition of tragedy. Noel Coward was in Durban, the guest in South Africa of General Smuts, and on the evening of 14 March 1944, after having given a concert in the City Hall, he was entertained by the Mayor, Mr. Rupert Ellis Brown. My daughter Joy and I were there among the guests and in the course of the evening Noel Coward asked to hear me sing. I responded with 'When They Sound the Last All Clear' and then though the party was at its height, I felt that I must leave. Joy shared this feeling though neither of us was able to pin-point the reasons for not wishing to share in the gaiety and the ebullient wit of Britain's most famous living playwright. That dull, aching, undefined depression was the prelude to a moment some two weeks later – 30 March – when in my town studio Joy brought me the news of Roy's death. His death had occurred on 14 March – the very day that we had had the premonition at the party. Completely numb, but without a tear, I remembered the phrases which sparkled through all his most recent letters to me – 'I couldn't be happier away from home than I am now . . .'; 'The men are in fine fettle and we get on even better with closer acquaintanceship . . .' 'Feeling very fit and at the top of my form. My platoon is No. 14 C Company – a splendid bunch of dyed-in-the-wool genuine Jocks and my sergeant is one of the oldest members of the battalion – a great man to have beside you in a scrap . . .'.

I looked back, just as all mothers do when faced by similar moments of deep personal grief, to happier days when Roy and his brother Barrie were growing up together in a light-hearted world as yet unblemished by the threat of war and all the tragedy it held in store. Roy and his brother Barrie – there was a year's difference in their ages – were inseparable. They went to the same schools together, played in the same rugby side, swam together for their school and, on leaving, both adopted the same careers – they went to the Witwatersrand to become learner mining officials at the Sub Nigel gold-mine. Roy was a brilliant all-round athlete, earning his school colours for rugby, swimming and athletics and was once described by the Natal *Mercury* as having had 'one of the finest schoolboy winning careers ever recorded in South Africa'.

Both he and Barrie were always full of activity and enthusiasm, as deeply devoted to all the members of the family as they were to them. When war came it was inevitable that they would both be among the very first to volunteer for service and that is precisely what happened – literally within hours of the announcement that South Africa was at war. Almost to a man the young learner officials at Sub Nigel mine were bombarding the Johannesburg Drill Hall to join up, fearing in their naïve enthusiasm that the war would be over before they had a chance of seeing any action.

Both Roy and Barrie joined 'A' Company of the 1st Transvaal Scottish and in due course they served through the Abyssinian campaign, in Eritrea and then in the Western Desert. Roy was seconded from his regiment only a short while before the Tobruk débâcle and was posted to the Royal Army Corps in Cairo to be trained as a tank instructor. Barrie remained with the Scottish, narrowly avoiding capture at Tobruk.

At the battle of El Alamein in which the Transvaal Scottish played a distinguished part, Barrie, I learnt from a letter from his company officer, Lieut. Barney Stirton, was a first-class soldier. After a night patrol into the heart of enemy-held territory, Lieut. Stirton wrote to me saying, 'Barrie is still going strong. He has always been the life and soul of the platoon and as brave as a lion in action. It is men like him I have to thank for the decoration I wear.'

After the victory at El Alamein the 1st South African Division was sent home on leave and on that never-to-be-forgotten day when the *Nieuw Amsterdam* sailed into Durban, her decks lined with wildly cheering South African troops, it was with great pride that I was standing at my place on the North Pier. Alongside me stood Roy. He had flown back from Cairo and joined me on my dawn mission of welcome. It was while he was on leave in Durban that Roy and his fiancée were married and he then flew back to the Middle East to learn a short time later that he had been selected to undergo a training course in Palestine for a commission in the British Army.

So it was that Roy joined the 6th Battalion, Black Watch, Royal Highland Regiment, and went with them to Italy. Now he was dead, but with my spirit strengthened by memories of him I said to a broken-hearted Joy, 'Darling, nothing can separate Roy from us'. That remains true to this day.

Misfortunes seem never to come singly and only ten days later my mother died – at 4.40 in the morning, quietly, with a soft sigh, leaving a never-to-be-filled gap in our intimate little world which for so long had known her as the personification of perfect wifehood, motherhood and a devoted servant of every good cause.

In that ten day period – between the two saddest personal losses I had suffered in my lifetime – a job remained to be done and on 5 April 1944, I was down at the docks, having received a telephone call to say that a troopship crowded with South Africans returning to the Italian front was due to sail. The biggest fear that I faced was self-pity. Would I be able to stand there, looking up at that sea of soldiers' faces and not see in every one of them a reminder of my Roy? And would I then be able to sing without choking with emotion?

I knew that I must go down to the docks and sing. My own belief in the duty that I was doing every time I sang to a ship imposed its own discipline and so I went down and sang, but before doing so I telephoned one of my dearest friends in Durban and asked her to pray for me to be given the strength to face the ordeal that confronted me. At the docks I looked at those soldiers and I realized that I could never have failed them. How many, I wondered, in those anonymous, serried ranks of young eager men, looking down on me and hanging on every note I sang, were destined never to return. That gave me the strength and though my heart was bursting I sang on and on, hardly conscious that all around me tears were streaming down the faces of the canteen helpers who knew of the burden that lay so heavily on me.

A few days later came the call to sing to another ship, this time the *Reina del Pacifico*, which had on board servicemen and women and children. I remember some little girls, their heads popping through the portholes, asking me to sing 'I'm Dreaming of a White Christmas'. I did so and they kept waving to me until their ship was out of sight.

Later in the day I sang to some men in the *Talma* and to the crews of two destroyers, HMS *Mayborough* and *Jasmine*, and while singing a gunner came to me and shook my hand, saying he thought I was the bravest woman in the world. He told me he had often been terrified of going back to sea but he would never be afraid again.

Messages of sympathy and masses of beautiful flowers poured in on me and wherever I went in the docks, warm friendly handshakes and simple sincere words helped to ease the pain and I was able to carry on singing without breaking down, though on many occasions I came close to it. When the second blow of my mother's death struck me, again there were flowers, again the sympathy, and still I carried on, relying on a Divine Providence that I would not fail. It was just at this time that I received a letter from Mrs. Wyn Nicholls of Durban, one which I treasure deeply. It confirmed – if I needed confirmation – that like any other soldier in the field the duty I had to do had to be done, without regard to personal considerations, however agonizing those might be.

'I want to tell you a little story which I feel might be of some comfort to you at this stage', she wrote:

'Some months ago we met a Royal Surgeon Commander who was stationed at the Naval Hospital at Assegai. One of the first things he asked was, "Who is the lady in white who sang to us when we arrived in Durban?" I told him.

'Four days after the news of your son's death was published in the newspapers he left Durban. His last words were: "Well, we won't have the Lady in White to bid us farewell, seeing that her son has just been killed.

'A few weeks later we received a letter from him saying that as the ship pulled out your glorious voice came across the water to them, and there was hardly a man on board who hadn't a tear in his eye. He said that an officer spoke for all of them when he said "God bless her – what guts!".'

I had in the meantime cabled my husband, Jack, in Italy with No. 2 Squadron, South African Air Force, telling him of Roy's death and some time afterwards he managed to obtain leave to visit Roy's grave. He had meagre information to go on. It lay, he knew, somewhere along Route 7, but search though he did he was unable to find it and eventually he enlisted the help of GHQ in Rome and was directed to Shipton Bridge. There he saw Roy's grave, with a simple wooden cross above it – one of a vast number of similar graves that made the Luiri Valley seem, Jack told me later, one vast Black Watch graveyard.

I was to make my first pilgrimage to Roy's grave in 1952, after having attended, in London, the wedding of my daughter, Joy, to Major Howard Liddiard, whom she had first met when he was with the South Wales Borderers taking part in the Madagascar invasion.

I was warned, both in London and Rome, that it was a difficult mission to undertake on my own but was determined to go even though it involved a journey by train, then by narrow gauge railway and finally by taxi, with the possibility of being stranded should the taxi driver, for any reason, refuse to wait at the cemetery to bring me back again.

But, as ever, kind friends were ready to help. Mr. C.H. Henderson, of the British Embassy in Rome, with whom I had been in touch through Toc H, and his wife, were extremely kind. He was on the station in Rome to meet me and almost the first person to telephone a welcome to me was General Everard Poole, the former commander of the 6th S.A. Division and now his country's Minister Plenipotentiary in Rome. There had been many wartime contacts with the general and in his lovely house in the suburbs of Rome he, his wife and I relived some of the stirring times we had known.

Roy's grave had been moved from Garigliano River to the Minturno British cemetery and it was here, having been driven the 250 miles by Mr. and Mrs. Henderson, that I stood at Roy's graveside. It was beautifully tended with lawns and roses in full bloom flowering between the headstones, which seemed to stretch interminably – a silent indictment of the crime of war.

Seven years later when returning to his grave as a member of the British Empire Service League War Graves pilgrimage, it was still as lovingly cared for as it had been when I first saw it. On this second pilgrimage I visited, as well, the grave of my brother, Karl, buried near Doullon near Amiens on the Somme. His grave is also deep in the countryside in most peaceful surroundings.

The memories of both my brother Karl and my son Roy are enshrined in Durban's Old Fort, originally a triangular laager and magazine built in 1842 at the time of the siege of Durban. The magazine of this famous old landmark was later converted into a very lovely chapel with stained-glass windows in memory of Munro, the youngest son of Mr. and Mrs. Andrew Hepburn, who died in action in France in the First World War. In this chapel is a tablet inscribed to the memory of Karl and just below was placed a second tablet to the memory of Roy. His brother, Barrie, unveiled it at a remembrance service that was conducted by the Rev. Peter Gordon, MBE, CF.

Roy's death on that March day in 1944, followed so soon by that of my mother, shattered me emotionally but, if anything, it drew me subconsciously closer, through the bonds of suffering that I now shared personally, to those many thousands of other innocent victims of the world tragedy. I threw myself with greater fervour than ever into my self-appointed task and was able to look back with a sense of deep spiritual contentment on the little comfort I was able to bring into the lives of our fighting men, especially those wounded or disabled.

9

The hospital ships

The hospital ships provided me with the most heart-rending moments in my dockside singing career.

To them I owed, I knew, a special duty, and before the war had ended I had sung to them on more than 300 occasions. The rigid security measures that were enforced at Durban – as elsewhere – to conceal the comings and goings of the convoys were relaxed in the case of hospital ships, for under the Geneva Convention, the enemy was informed officially of their movements to guarantee their safety from attack. So we always knew in advance when a hospital ship was expected and it became my invariable practice to be waiting, at dawn, at the end of the North Pier, to sing a song of greeting as one of the familiar white ships, with the huge red crosses on her sides and funnels, steamed through the harbour entrance.

What a cargo of sadness and tragedy each one carried. As I stood there waiting to raise my voice in song, my heart would contract with pity and I would have to steel myself to face, with an outward appearance of cheerfulness, the day that lay ahead. I was able to do so, knowing that my singing to those men conveyed to them the sense of gratitude that all ordinary men and women felt for the suffering they were enduring in the cause of freedom.

From the North Pier I would sing a greeting and then dash to the quayside to be waiting for the ship as it docked. It was a scene that never varied in its poignancy. There were the long lines of hospital trains that would take the wounded and sick to the various military hospitals that had been established in different parts of the country; there the voluntary canteen workers, ready to provide refreshments and comforts and, like me, putting on a false front of cheerfulness to face the sadness that would soon unfold before them.

The *Amra* known officially as 'Hospital ship No. 49', had been put into service by the British India Steamship Company on the Calcutta–Rangoon run only a short time before the outbreak of war and then turned over to the British Admiralty when hostilities started, to become a South African hospital ship. Her commanding officer was Lt.-Col. Henry Hemstead. I sang no fewer than 33 times to the *Amra* as she arrived and sailed from Durban on her errands of mercy, carrying throughout the war, it is estimated, a total of 30,000 patients from the battlefields to hospitals in South Africa. Some of the men were dreadfully wounded, particularly those who had been blown up in minefields; many limbless, but, miraculously, their voices were always firm and their eyes bright.

The frequency with which the hospital ships came into Durban resulted, naturally, in the crews and the medical staffs on board them becoming close acquaintances and I came to know the songs that they regarded as their favourites. Captain Murphy, for example, the genial Irish-Australian master of *Amra*, always wanted me to sing his particular favourite – not surprisingly – 'Waltzing Matilda'. Colonel Gerard, officer commanding the Netherlands Indies Hospital ship *Orange*, always insisted on 'Thanks For the Lovely Week-end'.

Colonel Gerard, a retired doctor, was living in Java when the war broke out and was appointed to the *Orange* almost immediately Holland entered the war. He left his wife and daughter in what he believed to be the comparative safety of Java, but was to have the shattering experience of

Hospital ship *Amra* March 1946. Her last 'load' home to Durban and almost ready to be handed back to her owners. Red crosses now painted out on funnel and ship's side but still conspicuous on superstructure.

The Lady-in-White in the Star & Garter Home and St Dunstan's – ('Journey's End' for so many of *Amra*'s passengers.)

learning that they had been taken prisoners when Japan came into the war and overran the country. For years he had no knowledge of their fate but it all ended happily. I was to learn from a letter he wrote to me after VJ Day that he and his family were reunited and living in The Hague.

Once a hospital ship had tied up I would spend most of the day singing requests – always, however, from the dockside, for though hospital ships were exempted from the security regulations which forbade a civilian aboard, my special pass that allowed me to come and go in the docks was too precious to think of jeopardizing it; which might have been the case if some officious individual saw me going up the gangplank of one of the hospital ships.

Once the patients had been put aboard the hospital trains, however, I would go from carriage to carriage to sing the songs asked by those who were confined to their beds.

Blindness, one of the most terrible of war's afflictions, was the fate that befell an old friend of our family, Morgan Edward 'Bill' Barrett. He returned to Durban in the *Amra*, and speaking with him, he asked me about a picture he had seen me paint of begonias some years previously. He loved that picture, which was later bought by Lady Duncan, wife of Sir Patrick Duncan, a Governor-General of South Africa, and subsequently hung in Libertas, the official home of General Smuts.

Such is the recuperative powers of the spirit that 'Bill', who believed that his life was for ever blighted when his world was plunged into eternal darkness, readapted himself and in 1942 married the girl who had nursed him and returned with her to his farm in the Orange Free State. The last time I saw him it was difficult to realize that he was blind. He rode a horse, supervised the running of the farm and was leading a contented family life surrounded by his wife, Peace, and their two children. Peace one day said,

'Our little girl is his eyes. As Bill canters over the farm his horse follows hers.'

Another memory of the *Amra* was dazzled by the loudest dressing-gown I had ever seen in my life – a violent combination of puce and yellow. it was worn by 'Young Jimmy' of the Royal Navy, a submariner who had 'liberated' it from a Nazi sailor. 'Young Jimmy' did lots for our morale, recounting incidents in which they had sunk 12 enemy ships in 17 days, and sending to the bottom, as well, an Italian submarine off the Greek coast. I was never able to establish whether all that 'Young Jimmy' told us was strictly accurate, but in those grim days, when one Allied bastion after another was falling before the Nazi onslaught, his stories were music to our ears.

Despite the Geneva Convention and the protection it was supposed to afford to hospital ships it was not always observed. I was told a horrifying story by the veteran chief petty officer of the *Amra* of how, when he was serving aboard another hospital ship taking wounded troops from Tobruk, German Stuka dive-bombers attacked the ship, scoring direct hits. The patients in the now badly damaged hospital ship were transferred to a British destroyer which had come alongside, but the transfer had to be accomplished over narrow planks across which the patients, many of them seriously wounded, had to walk. They did so, each man walking alone along the narrow planks rising and falling with the motion the sea, until all were safely aboard the destroyer. He had never seen men so calm, the chief petty officer told me. The hospital ship limped back into Tobruk Harbour for repairs only to suffer, later in the war, another attack by German bombers.

I have, and treasure, a tangible momento of the *Amra*, a gold filigree ring presented to me by the orderlies of the ship.

When on 2 May I took up my dawn position on the North Pier to welcome the hospital ship *Vita*, it was a glorious morning, the sky diffused with a soft light that Turner would have revelled in capturing on canvas. But my thoughts were concentrated on the *Vita*, for she carried that day one of the saddest cargoes of the war – the survivors – most of them terribly burned – of HMS *Cornwall* and *Dorsetshire*, sunk on Easter Sunday, 5 April 1942, off Colombo by Japanese dive-bombers. The cruiser *Dorsetshire* is for ever enshrined in the annals of British naval history by reason of the fact that it was she who delivered the *coup de grâce* to the German raider *Bismarck* – at the time of her sinking one of the most powerful battleships in the world and constituting one of the gravest threats to Britain's life-lines. Torpedoes from HMS *Dorsetshire* repeatedly hit the German raider and at 10.40 on that morning of 27 May 1941 the great ship turned over and foundered in the icy waters of the North Sea.

In 1942, transferred to the Far East to help stem the onrushing Japanese tidal wave HMS *Dorsetshire*, commanded by the great and gallant Captain A.W. Shelton Agar, VC, sailed from Colombo with HMS *Cornwall* to join the main fleet then steaming to engage the Japanese fleet heading for Colombo. The day was calm and clear when suddenly from out of the sky the attack burst on the two ships in a crescendo of violence. Waves of dive-bombers followed each other in formations of three at intervals of a few seconds. In a little more than 15 minutes both cruisers had been sunk. The survivors clung to floating wreckage and faced with fortitude the ordeal of waiting for the rescue which all knew must be long. In all, 1,122 officers and men from the two ships, many of them badly wounded and burned, were picked up the following evening by HMS *Enterprise* and two destroyers, after enduring 30 hours under a tropical sun in shark infested waters; 29 officers and 395 men perished. Among the survivors was Captain Agar, who went so deep into the water as his ship sank that he burst a lung. When he came up to the surface he managed to swim to a raft which had remained afloat and then, aware that the mortal enemy that they now had to face was sharks, he ordered the sailors floundering in the water to form a vast circle. In the centre were the wounded and the bodies of the men killed or drowned. The men clung together, hand to hand, until 30 hours later HMS *Enterprise* and the destroyers arrived.

I recently received a letter from Captain Agar to tell me that he was improving in health and to thank me for all I had done for the morale of his men on that day the *Vita* steamed into Durban harbour.

Also among the *Cornwall* survivors was Able Seaman Harold 'Paddy' Keeping, of Maidstone, Kent, blinded in both eyes and doomed, the doctors believed, never to see again. While in hospital in Durban, however, he accidentally struck his head hard against the bedpost and to his amazement discovered that he could see again. 'I can see – I can see'. He kept shouting as the doctors and nurses came running. His eyesight was restored on the very day they were going to give him a braille watch.

Like the other hospital ships the *Vita* was a frequent visitor to Durban and I formed a warm friendship with three Royal Navy signalmen, John Turnbull, Denis Ward and Bob Patrick Walker, whom I nicknamed 'Rufus' for he had a magnificent pointed red beard and looked every inch the traditional British salt. All three paid many visits to Pineholme and I did a life-sized portrait of the bearded Rufus which, before I sent it to him, was on view at the Natal Society of Artists' exhibition, which was opened by Admiral Sir Desmond McCarthy, C-in-C. South Atlantic.

From the:
66
EASTER 1971.

Taken from the text of the *Shire Times* (HMS *Dorsetshire* Ass. Magazine):
Once a year we try to assemble and pay homage to our old ship and to our long lost, but never forgotten, shipmates.

The thatch has thinned, some of us have already started to use a razor and many a linnet has roosted in the old 'crow's nest'.

We now have the foundations of a really grand fellowship laid, don't let us lapse through apathy as a lot of these societies have done.

Extract from BBC (Forces) Programme broadcast on September 15 1942 at 9.25p.m. Mr A.C. Elsgood's version (Canteen Manager) on the sinking of the *Dorsetshire*:
'Then someone cried they could see smoke in the distance. Within one hour of seeing that smoke I was hauled aboard a destroyer. I remembered my thoughts the day before about having something new for Easter. Mine turned out to be a new experience, a thirty hour bath in the Indian Ocean.

But, I thought, I've had a present too – I've seen my fellow Britons at their splendid best, indomitably cheerful and sustaining each other to the end against the worst kind of ordeal.

And that, I shall always remember.'

Requiem
'Shrouded in flames and acrid smoke billowing, many muffled external explosions, to the accompaniment of the shrieking siren screaming defiance, the ten thousand tons of tortured metal slowed up-ended and with ever increasing speed, slid into the watery depths.

Huge bubbles appeared, some puny humans with them, and then silence except for the cries of the infused and helping shipmates.
We were alone.'

The Lady in White standing on Plymouth Hoe 3rd April 1970 when she was guest of the *HMS Dorsetshire* Survivors' Association Reunion a year before she died.

The *Vita* had, perhaps, the most adventurous wartime career of all the hospital ships. She happened to be close at hand at the time the aircraft carrier *Hermes* was sunk off Ceylon and succeeded in rescuing 590 of the crew – all of whom, in due course, were brought to Durban. I have a graphic photograph, given to me by John Turnbull, showing the *Hermes* survivors swimming in the sea – some in life-jackets, others clinging to rafts.

The sight of grievously wounded and mutilated men was always a moving and tragic spectacle but, if anything, even more sad were those cases, on board every hospital ship, of men whose bodies were untouched but whose minds had been shattered by the stress of war. I was to be told, many years after the war had ended, of a young British officer who, being brought to Durban in the *Amra* was so violent and struggled with such maniacal force that it was decided he be placed in a strait-jacket. The orderlies were engaged in a terrific struggle to control him while the jacket was being put on, the officer screaming and foaming at the mouth. In the midst of this terrible scene one of the orderlies told me, my voice singing 'There'll Always Be an England' was suddenly heard, clear as a bell above the frenzied din and the effect was miraculous.

'One moment', said the orderly, 'we had a lunatic on our hands. In the next he had stopped struggling and was listening intently to your singing. He even motioned to us in the cabin to keep quiet. He became normal in seconds and was completely relaxed. He dressed himself and asked permission to go on deck so that he could see you, and then, having looked at you standing there on the dockside singing, he remained completely relaxed. On the long journey to Johannesburg, to the Baragwanath Military Hospital, he never gave us a moment's trouble. He spoke constantly of you and your singing. You did a wonderful job that day. It was something the other orderlies and I will never forget.'

As the war progressed South Africa became the main hospital and convalescent centre for the British forces and great hospitals were opened in Natal and elsewhere in the country to care for the wounded and ill. I was invited by Surgeon Rear-Admiral Hobbs, RN, to sing at the hospitals which were fairly close to Durban and devoted Fridays of every week to paying regular visits to the naval hospital at Wentworth. I would begin singing at 2pm and finish at about 6.30. Once, while singing to a ward filled with sick men, a worried doctor and matron came in and told me that it was a TB ward, with none of the patients being allowed out or to mix with other patients for fear that they would spread the disease.

'Are you afraid of infection?' the doctor asked. I was not, he was told, and from that day the TB wards were never omitted from my singing rounds. Later with the help of members of a singing club I had established in Durban for young business girls, evening concerts were regularly given to the TB patients. As a further lift to their morale I suggested to the girls that they wear gay evening frocks on these singing occasions. The impact this had on the men was remarkable. They had become accustomed to seeing girls in uniform only – some of the men had not been outside the wards for two years or more – but now they were seeing again vivid reminders of their happy pre-war years. Eventually, the rigid policy towards TB patients was relaxed and it became possible for me to invite groups of them to Pineholme for parties in the garden.

When the hospital ship *Tairea* arrived in Durban in June 1942 I was, as usual, singing on the quayside as the men were being carried from the ship to the trains, when a nurse came and said that a blind man in the train had asked to see me. He was Jimmy Ellis, a cavalry officer to the 10th Hussars, who had lost his sight and had had his left hand and two fingers of his right hand amputated as a result of having been blown up in a minefield in the Western Desert. He asked me to sing to him – which I did softly and gently – while sitting on the edge of his bed. As I sang he held my hand so tightly with his remaining fingers that it almost hurt.

He told me that he used to play the piano and I could sense his sad, unspoken realization that never again would that pleasure be his. The train took him away to hospital, but I often thought of him and wondered how he had adjusted to his affliction. Then, some years after the war ended, I answered the telephone to hear a man's voice say, 'You won't remember me, but my name is Jimmy Ellis. You sang to me years ago and I so much want to see you.'

We met and he filled in the period since that last meeting so long ago. For eighteen months he remained in hospital in South Africa and was then sent to St. Dunstan's in England to undergo training in some trade. There they found, however, that he had a natural ability as a speaker and he became an appeals organizer, travelling around the country raising funds for the society. The realization that he was able, despite his handicap, to do a worthwhile job and to do it well gave him great spiritual strength and he took a step which he had long avoided, fearing a rebuff.

He wrote to a girl in South Africa and asked her to marry him. They had met at a hospital dance in Cape Town while he was awaiting the ship that would take him back to England and the St. Dunstan's training centre. She was a nurse and asked him to dance.

'Oh, no I can't', he protested.

'Come on! You never will if you don't try.'

They danced. He never lost touch with her again after that and when he had completed his training and was confident in his new-found strength he proposed to her. They married, toured England together and some years later they came back to South Africa – he as the appeals organizer in South Africa for St. Dunstan's, she to run their home and family of two delightful daughters. I found out, too, that he had even managed to play the piano again with his few remaining fingers. I made this discovery when at a function to celebrate the presentation of a large cheque by the Durban branch of St. Dunstan's to the funds of the National Council for the Blind. Jimmy was there and he sat down at the piano and played. I was to marvel again, as I have marvelled so often, how man is able to triumph over adversity.

I was, of course, to come into contact with a great many nurses of many different nationalities who served in the hospital ships, and found that common to every one of them was their deep devotion to the sick and wounded. I remember, in particular, Sister Eleanor Savage who, serving first in the *Orange* and then in the *Centaur*, was the acknowledged heroine when her hospital ship was sunk by the Japanese and, though she had three broken ribs, she tended to and prayed over a man dying of burns and kept the spirits up of the other terribly wounded men.

Then there was small, dark-haired Yeske Vestdik, a Dutch nurse on board the *Orange* who, escaping first from Holland when the Germans overran her country, found herself again faced with having to flee from the Japanese troops advancing on Java where she was living. Escape she did in a Netherlands minesweeper that had been camouflaged to resemble an island. The captain of the minesweeper, having wounded naval men on board, with no one to care for them, asked for volunteers and found an immediate response from Yeske. She joined the ship in Surabaya harbour, already littered with the hulks of bombed and scuttled ships, and cared for the wounded, while the crew first skilfully covered the superstructure of the ship with boughs and branches of trees to make it indistinguishable to prowling Japanese aircraft, and then slipped it out of the harbour under the cover of night. It reached Australia safely where Yeske joined the *Orange*.

Matron 'Bloody Bill' Hawkins occupies a special place in the saga of wartime nurses. She was the first matron of the Children's Hospital in Durban and, as my mother was instrumental in having the hospital established, Matron Hawkins was naturally a close and valued friend of ours. She volunteered for service in World War II and served both in East Africa and the Middle East, being in charge, at one time, of No. 4 General Hospital after the fall of Tobruk. Her somewhat unflattering nickname was given by her staff who, while they loved her and would do anything for her, were under no illusions as to her fire-eating disposition when matters of discipline were involved.

Men who are badly wounded or desperately ill react with far deeper emotions than their healthy counterparts, and it was not surprising, therefore, that a great many of the men who came to thank me after the war were those who remembered hearing me singing from the beds in which they were lying as patients. One such caller in June 1947, was Captain John Williams, of the Welsh Guards, who recalled how, having heard me sing when he was in the troopship *Maloja* on his way to the Far East, heard my voice again when he returned to Durban as patient in the hospital ship *Tjitjalengka*. He had been through the Burma campaign and had been wounded twice, had had malaria and dysentry, with his life despaired of by the doctors. He was lying in his bunk in the hospital train when I arrived with my arms filled with roses. The previous day some of the patients in the *Tjitjalengka* asked me to sing 'The Last Rose of Summer' and I, puzzled by their request, asked them why they wanted that song in particular. Because, they said, it was seven years since they had last seen a rose and the song, therefore, had special sentimental connotations. I sang the song they wanted and early the following morning collected all the roses I could and took them down to the docks where the patients were being transferred to the hospital trains. As I went through the carriages some of the patients buried their faces in the roses and tears streamed unashamedly down their faces. This was the occasion Captain Williams recalled for me.

In the bunk below Captain Williams lay Dr. Prothero, who earlier had wanted me to speak to him but who, when I reached him that morning, was too ill to say anything. He had lost his power of speech through shock, privation and brutal treatment by the Japanese.

While it was I who most often did the singing there was an occasion when the procedure was reversed. On board the hospital ship *Aba* when it came into Durban in August in 1941 was a young blinded soldier whom I was to know only as Dudley. I was singing to the patients in the waiting hospital train when Dudley asked for me. He was leaning out of the carriage window as I came up and sang the song 'Pola' to me, only he changed the name 'Pola' to 'Perla' so that it went like this:

> 'Oh, my Perla,
> That pretty little poppy, must copy
> It's endearing charms from you.'

— 10 —

Stars and Stripes

I had often wondered how long it would be before my dockside repertoire would include such songs as 'Over There' 'The Star Spangled Banner', 'Yankee Doodle' and other American favourites. The United States, at war since December 1941, was girding her vast and powerful resources to throw in on the side of freedom, but it was not before 30 October 1942 that we were to see for the first time in Durban the Stars and Stripes flying from a group of destroyers that were escorting the *Mauretania*, crammed with American troops bound for the Far East. The *Mauretania* was berthed alongside the *Nieuw Amsterdam*, to which, on the following day, I was singing when from the American troopship came the cry 'Hey, Ma . . . , what about us?' I asked them what they wanted and with one voice they replied 'The Shores of Tripoli'. I had to confess that I didn't know the words of that stirring fighting song and the Americans there and then decided to bring my education up to date. A group of US Marines surrounded me, and while some taught me the tune, others wrote down the verses. The *Mauretania* sailed on 3 November and from the North Pier I sang them their favourite song – word perfect.

More and more American troopships began visiting Durban from this time on and I increased my repertoire to include 'God Bless America', one song which always had a most moving effect on us US troops. I sang it for the first time to the *Orantjes* when it sailed on 7 June 1943, laden with troops and nurses, and thereafter I never failed to sing it to any ship flying the Stars and Stripes.

Aware though I was of the efficiency of American publicity methods, I was startled at the rapidity with which my existence became so widely known throughout the United States, and the effect it had on that most sentimental of nations. It started when *Time* magazine in 1943 made mention of my dockside singing, saying that to the US doughboys I was known as Kate Smith or the Dockside Diva; to Britons as the Lady in White, or the soldier's sweetheart, and to the Poles as the South African Nightingale.

This was followed by an article in *Life* magazine which, under the heading of 'Dockside Diva', called me a 'streamlined Kate Smith', and went on to describe my daily practice of going down to the docks to sing to arriving and departing ships. My morale-building value was rated as 'high' by the naval authorities, said the article, which added: 'At first when the ship is untied the men join in so heartily that when an onshore breeze is blowing the song feast can be heard in Central Durban, a mile away. But by the time the ship is over the bar Perla is singing alone. Farewells are always charged by misty-eyed emotion on both sides . . . .'

The *Life* article had many repercussions. I was made an honorary member of an organization known as the International Magna Carta Day Association, dedicated to the promotion of unity among English-speaking nations. I received a letter from the executive secretary, Mr J.W. Hamilton, of New York, who wrote:

'We are all charmed to read the account of your splendid activities, and I am sure that a million of our men and yours rise up and call you blessed every time they hear any woman sing.

'We are happy to enclose the article from *Life*; though no doubt you will get others, for many of our 20,000,000

Aboard USS *Speigel Grove*, Flagship of Rear Admiral Fluckey, US Navy 22 May 1961.

A family reunion

On the back of this photo Perla had written 'I was telling Monty that the last Press photo I'd seen of him was at the Albert Hall El Alamein Rally with the arms of Marlene Dietrich around his neck!'

of the Magna Carta Day Association who read *Life*, will have the happy thought to send it on to you.

'Our folder is enclosed; also "The Processional of the Seven Nations" which has been sung far and wide for ten years. The music suggested is grand, and the words are most popular, being sung in cathedrals, churches and so on in many parts of the world.

'Will you honour us by accepting an Honorary Membership in our Association?'

Though this was 1944 and political differences with Russia had not yet emerged with such terrifying possibilities, the Association's letter added that the statesmen of the free nations of the world were concerned by Russia's behaviour and that 'it becomes all the more necessary for our nations to close ranks. The pillars of human freedom rest upon the shoulders of our English-speaking nations.'

The 'Processional of the Seven Nations' was only one of several songs that I received from America.

A Mr. C.E. Grant sent me a song entitled 'O God of Heaven', saying in his letter to me:

'As a veteran of the First World War, I feel that war can never stop war. I have written this hymn in an effort to put into words my feeling and desire for the entire world.'

The first verse went:

'O God of Heaven, O King of earth, our
   supplications rise
For all our armed forces, on land, on sea, in skies,
That by Thy mighty love and power wherever
   they may be,

> They shall be free from every foe, and own and
> worship thee.'

And from Winnipeg, Canada, a Mr. P.J. Fowler, who fought
in the South African War, sent me another song, writing:

> 'Up here in faraway Winnipeg we have read about the
> wonderful work you are doing, meeting and greeting
> the soldiers of the Allies on their journey to far
> horizons. It must certainly be a unique experience to
> hear your songs as the boats leave for mysterious ports.
>
> 'I do not know if many men from Western Canada
> have passed through Durban, but I am sending you a
> song – 'March on to Victory', which many men of the
> Canadian prairies know. It was written and composed
> by two Winnipeg musicians. One of them, Gordon
> McLean, is now with the 'Canada Show' in England.
>
> 'You may find this song a suitable and inspiring one
> to add to your extensive repertoire. In any case, please
> accept the song with the warmest wishes of Western
> Canada and a hope that you will go on singing to the
> boys and girls until the victorious end.'

One of the most moving letters I received was from Mr. A.C.
Mullock, Clerk and Treasurer of the township of East
Flamboro, Waterdown, Ontario, who wrote:

> 'Perhaps it is a little late to thank you, but in 1943 a very
> close friend of mine, Ron, sailed away from your port
> and wrote to me of the lady who sang as the boat
> pulled out. He was deeply moved and wrote to me at
> the time to tell me about it, and how he planned to
> thank you in person when he came back. But that was
> not to be and now I want to say thanks for him for

something that he said he would never forget.

'Thanks again for Ron. It made him happy and thanks also from me as Ron's friend, as he only deserved the best that any of us had to offer.'

A letter I received from Mr. A.E. Shulson, of Lake Shore Boulevard, Cleveland, Ohio, was accompanied by a parcel of chewing-gum, a gift that was prompted by his having read in the *Life* article that on the first occasion US troops sailed into Durban they threw their precious chewing-gum to me. I promptly sent it up in a gift parcel to my sons in the Middle East. 'Anyone who helps the boys is a friend of mine and a friend of America', wrote Mr. Shulson. 'The enclosed package of gum is not much, but after reading the *Life* article, I said to myself – will get myself some gum and mail it to her so that she can send it to her boys. May the Good Father spare them.'

I was to receive direct news of my American uncle, Ted, whom I had visited in New York before the First World War when he was Technical Director of the Metropolitan Opera House. Mr. Byron R. Keller, a member of the American Field Service, was, in peacetime, a producer on the staff of the Metropolitan Opera, and in addition to giving me news about my uncle, he told me that he had first heard of me from soldiers serving in Burma. Knowing my father's brother as he did, he was practically a member of the family and we had some delightful evenings together at Pineholme singing Hebridean folk-songs, on which many of the Negro spirituals are based.

Byron Kelly sailed from Durban in a new American tanker, the *Wolfe Creek*, to which I sang good-bye as it left.

The military authorities just about this time relaxed their rigidly enforced regulations, and permitted me to paint in the dock area, subject to all my paintings being submitted for censorship. The first ship I painted happened to be an American one – an extremely unusual one in the year 1944. It was, of all things, a three-masted sailing ship, which limped into harbour for repairs in October that year.

My wartime undertaking to sing to the Navy whenever it visited Durban was automatically extended to include the US Navy, and in November 1948 I was at my place at dawn on the North Pier to welcome the American light cruiser *Huntington*, and the destroyer *Douglas H. Fox*. It was pouring with rain as I stood there wrapped in a man's macintosh singing through my megaphone 'God Bless America', then to listen to the American ships returning the complement by having their band play 'Sarie Marais'. A Durban newspaper produced a picture of me the next day damply standing there singing in the rain, and made the suggestion that Durban was failing in her famed reputation for hospitality by allowing American naval vessels to sail into the harbour with only a single person there to welcome them. In view of the weather their reluctance to wait at the docks was understandable, but the newspaper's comment touched Durbanite consciences, and they then gave the American visitors a great reception.

It rained solidly for four days while the Americans were in port, and an incident occurred which had a somewhat dampening effect on the warm welcome we had prepared at Pineholme for Captains Lindsay and Ashleigh Burke, of the two US ships. They stepped out of their car outside Pineholme into a storm-water drain, up to their waists in water.

Canada was already a geographic part of my repertoire when in 1944 I sang 'Maple Leaf' as a farewell to the sentimental Canadian padre on board the aircraft carrier HMS *Atholrig*. There had arrived in South Africa some time earlier 300 Canadian nurses who, with nurses from other parts of the Commonwealth, were sent to South Africa to staff the many great hospitals that had come into being when it was decided that South Africa should become the medical half-way house between the battlefronts both of the Far East and the Middle East and Britain. Many of those Canadian nurses married South Africans and remain in the country to this day.

Those who returned home never forgot their stay in South Africa. They formed an organization to keep in touch with each other and to recall their wartime life in South Africa. They even produced their own newspaper, in one issue of which they made nostalgic mention of the 'Lady in White'.

No one at that time, when the war in Europe was drawing at last to its end, knew how many months – or years – would be required to extinguish the martial ardour of the fanatical Japanese, though none doubted the final outcome. The atomic bomb hadn't even been whispered of. And so, we in Durban, as the final act in the European drama was being mounted, turned our thoughts and energies to the problems we would face as the ships representing vast, invincible might of the United Nations, set themselves to the task of destroying the Japanese war machine. The announcement of VE day had set in train tremendous celebrations, but any tendency to relax our efforts, to yield to the luxury of complacency, was dispelled by the thunderous words of Sir Winston Churchill in a broadcast to the world on 13 May 1945. 'I told you hard things at the beginning of these last five years', he said. 'You did not shrink, and I should be unworthy of your confidence and generosity if I did not still cry: Forward, unflinching, unswerving, indomitable, till the whole task is done and the whole world is safe and clean.'

HMS HOWE

The 1945 painting described by Perla on page 83 still hangs in Lord Curzon's ancestral home at Amersham, Bucks. Permission was given by the current incumbent, cousin of he who bought it originally, for Chris Floyd – a freelance photographer – to call in February 1991 and take a photograph for this book.

When mutiny threatened

And so, with the war in Europe at long last at its victorious end, but the task of defeating Japan remaining, Durban harbour carried on unchanged: security measures were enforced as strictly as ever, ships came and went, their movements cloaked in secrecy. But there was a marked lessening in tension and the life of the voluntary workers took on a less hectic pace. I continued to come and go at will in the harbour area – be it at midnight or the first light of dawn – the first woman ever accorded such a privilege by the British Admiralty. I guarded that right jealousy and never infringed a single regulation. I never asked questions or ever spoke about ships or shipping, and never discussed many of the strange happenings witnessed in the course of my years of intimate wartime contact with the docks. Now, as I look back, I can recall many movements of high drama, some of them that threatened to involve that most heinous of naval sins – mutiny on the high seas.

Condemnations of those who in wartime even thought of rebelling against discipline comes easy, but it must, in justice, be considered against the background of appalling conditions that many men endured aboard the troopships on their long journeys to the battlefronts. With the free world so perilously short of merchant shipping through enemy sinkings, many of the troopships had to be packed with four or even five times their normal passenger capacity. The men suffered intensely from their close confinement, especially in the blazing tropical heat and from all the attendant discomforts of sleepless nights, sweltering in bunks in the blacked-out holds below the waterline; queuing interminably for meals and, pressing on their emotions, the all-pervading fear that at any moment an unseen enemy might strike from beneath the sea.

It is not surprising, then, that there were occasions when troops came close to mutiny. To me the wonder of it is that so many millions of men accepted their wartime fate with such equanimity.

The first such situation occurred in March 1942, but it was not until three days after the convoy had sailed into Durban that I was even aware of the drama that was being played out in one of the ships. I had sung as usual to the nine ships as they passed by the North Pier in the early morning and had received the usual warm reception from the men lining the decks. To me there seemed nothing untoward. But three days later, when I was in the canteen a group of military policemen, G.A. Gainham of Southampton, A.H. Trickett of Sheffield, H. Smith of London, C.A. Potts of Greenford, S.A. Fox of Norwich, C. Fox of Doncaster, and N. Cransley of Blackpool, asked to see me. They wanted to thank me, they said, for preventing what had every indication of being an extremely ugly situation developing on board their ship, as it was coming into the harbour. Many of the troops, sickened and weary of the long journey and uncomfortable conditions, threatened that they would walk off the ship the moment it docked. No amount of pleading or threats of disciplinary action against them appeared to have any effect, and the officers were gravely concerned at what might happen, and the disastrous consequences that conceivably could flow from precipitate action by the disaffected men. The ship was passing through the harbour entrance, one of the Red Caps told me, when suddenly a loud cooee was heard, followed by a voice singing 'Land of Hope and Glory' and then 'There'll Always Be an England'.

'The effect was miraculous,' he went on, 'everyone on board seemed suddenly to relax. The mood changed from sullen resentment to cheerfulness in minutes and soon the men were singing lustily with you. We, braced for what we fully expected was to be one of the toughest spells ever spent ashore, found ourselves dealing with men who behaved like lambs.'

The deputation brought with them a camera and asked to take my picture as a memento of what to them was a memorable occasion. They were going to send a copy of the photograph from whichever was their next port of call but I never received it. It was just about the time of the fall of Singapore. Were they among the victims, I have often wondered? I do, however, retain a memento of the occasion – a signed letter of thanks from the seven MPs.

Later in the war a ship laden with Australians for the Middle East radioed ahead of its arrival in Durban requesting that military police stand by when the ship docked to deal with a situation that might arise as a result of some of the troops being 'restless'. I sang 'Waltzing Matilda' as the ship came in, totally unaware of anything amiss. The first inkling that something unusual was happening was when we were told to close down our canteen temporarily – the ship was to be berthed near by – and then we noticed an unusually large contingent of military police on the quayside. The moment the ship was alongside the commanding officer came ashore to meet a group of high-ranking military officers and port officials and they held a hurried meeting behind the closed doors of the canteen. When they came out we were told to reopen the canteen and while that was being done one of the port officials came over saying 'Good work, Perla'. I asked what he meant and he told of the radio message received from the ship's captain, and that a grave situation was expected to arise when the ship docked. My singing had, however, changed the mood of the men and by the time the ship was alongside the quay the resentment harboured by the troops evaporated. 'As far as the OC is concerned, 'said the port official, 'you are his pin-up girl.'

After the war I was to learn of another occasion when near mutiny threatened in a ship crowded with African troops returning from the Middle East. I was being formally presented with the Certificate of Commendation bestowed on me by King George VI, and, in making the presentation, Senator Colonel ET Stubbs recounted to the Press an incident which had happened while the Middle East campaign was still in progress.

Some misunderstanding had arisen in Egypt about home leave and there had been wild demonstrations by the African troops, who considered themselves victims of an injustice. The long journey home did nothing to improve their tempers and Durban was warned in advance to expect trouble when the ships carrying them docked. More than 400 policemen were stationed in the sheds ready for instant action if the attempts at conciliation made by Colonel Stubbs failed and the African troops showed signs of getting out of hand.

Colonel Stubbs, to his surprise, found instead of an explosive situation thousands of Africans delighted to be home and completely disciplined in their behaviour. They had heard me singing as the ships sailed in and this, it seemed, once again had a magical calming effect.

Only once, to my knowledge, did men actually walk off a ship in Durban in protest. It was in August 1942, when members of the RAF on board the *Woodlark* were so disgruntled with their conditions that shortly before the ship was due to sail, they marched off in protest. I never heard the sequel to that incident as, in accordance with my policy, I never inquired.

I was, as I have said, never aware of these situations existing until the danger of the explosion was all over. But on one occasion I was to experience at first hand mass hysteria gripping a crowd. It was on 15 June 1942, at Maydon Wharf. Contingents of South African troops were embarking in the *Empire Success*, which was to take them to the Middle East, and, as usual, huge crowds of civilians had come to the docks to see them off. Unlike other, more concentrated, areas of Durbans's docks, Maydon Wharf had so many roads leading to the warehouses that it would have been impossible to cordon off the area completely with barbed wire. As Ian Findlay, of the RAF, and I were making our way towards Maydon Wharf we could hear excited shouting and yelling and we saw that a large number of women – wives, mothers and sweethearts – standing behind the barbed-wire fence had been completely carried away emotionally and were straining against the fence disregarding the warnings of two old soldiers, veterans of the Boer War, who were guarding the area. From the ships soldiers were shouting 'break the fence down – they won't shoot you'. It was a situation fraught with danger, for if those hysterical, overwrought women had indeed taken the irresponsible advice being shouted to them, there would have been certain tragedy. Many would have been pushed over the quayside into the sea. One of the old soldier guards, seeing me, urged me to try to do something to calm the women. I took a deep breath and, shouting as loudly as I could, I said, 'Please, everyone, be quiet. It's hard enough for your men to leave. It is up to us to try to make things easier for them – not more difficult. Stop it, don't let them down. Let's give them a song instead.' And with that I started to sing 'Wish Me Luck as You Wave Me Goodbye'. A few women joined me, then a few more and soon that whole crowd was singing. I kept singing until the ship cast off and had disappeared round 'T' jetty and out to sea.

The effect of my welcoming songs on the morale of men, desperate after long weeks at sea, was described in a book *Absence Without Leave*, by Allan Jenkins. A note in the front of the book declared that all the characters in the story and their names were fictitious and that no reference was made or intended to any actual person – living or dead. It left me with a somewhat eerie feeling to see myself accurately described in one passage in the book.

The particular excerpt read:

'Suddenly a woman began to sing. The troops strained their necks to see who it was and gave a gentle ironical cheer. The voice swelled into "Land of Hope and Glory". Silence fell upon the troops and those on the dockside. All you could hear was the clank and hiss of cranes and winches and the woman singing. Her voice was rich, rotund, firm as a rock. She was the mother of all men. Her voice embraced them in a bear-hug and wrung tears from them.

'"There she is". Fingers pointed to an ample white figure on the quayside. Nick Riskin [the hero], struggling for a glimpse of her, felt his throat contract. They seemed to like soldiers here. God, God, I'm proud to be in the army. This will never do. . . .

'The troops, hypnotized, joined in the refrain. The plump woman in white smiled maternally and beat time with a purple bandana in her hand. The quayside chorus rose to a climax and dissolved in a fury of cheering. The woman in white was still singing, but the ship had passed her by now, and her voice came faintly over the water: "There'll Always Be an England", "Sally", "The Last All-Clear", "Old Father Thames".

'She was an outpost of Britain, South Africa's loyalty, symbol of the Empire family.

'"Give us another, Ma", the men shouted hoarsely. They swayed to the rhythm. An hour ago they'd been mutinous with impatience to get ashore, jumpy and embittered by weeks of discomfort, half-pay, short rations. They hadn't cared a damn where they were going, whom or why they were going to fight. Now, incredibly, someone was glad to see them.'

There were, of course, many lighter dockside moments – and even several romantic interludes. Once, as a number troopships with South Africans aboard were preparing to sail, we were surprised to see a motor-car, escorted by military police on motor-cycles, sweep up to the quayside and stop a short distance from one of the ships. A man emerged from the car, hurried over to the gangplank and spoke earnestly for a few minutes to the guard on duty. Soon afterwards the ship's tannoy blared, calling for Private . . . to report immediately to the gangway.

In the meantime a middle-aged woman, a girl who was obviously her daughter, and a minister left the car and were waiting at the foot of the gangway. Soon afterwards a soldier, looking acutely embarrassed, came down the gangway to be warmly embraced by the girl. I, who was standing near, heard the girl's excited voice saying something about 'marriage – isn't it wonderful'. The soldier, conscious of the eyes of thousands of his comrades firmly fixed on him, quite obviously had mixed feelings at that moment but one thing he made clear. He wasn't intending to get married in full view of thousands of cynical soldiers. So the whole wedding party transferred itself to one of the goods sheds and there, in the gloom and amid all the crates and with the throb and clatter of cranes and railway trucks the couple were married. The berthing master, Mr. Viljoen, was one of the witnesses and he claimed his traditional right of kissing the bride. There was a hurried farewell embrace by the young bride and bridegroom and then the soldier dashed back to the gangway to board the crowded troopship in which he would spend his 'honeymoon'.

Soon after the war's end I played a more active role as Cupid when the troopship *Felix Roussel* sailed into Durban bringing South Africans back home. A pretty, shy young girl came up to me in the dock area and asked if she might stand alongside me as I sang a welcome to the incoming ship. Her fiancée was aboard, she told me, adding that she had never seen him, nor had he seen her in the flesh. Their romance had started and blossomed entirely by correspondence, and now that he was on his way home they were faced with the dilemma of identifying each other with the least possible delay. The enterprising young girl had come up with the solution. She wrote to her soldier boyfriend telling him that I was always at my place on the North Pier singing welcome to the ships and that as she was sure I would be there when his ship came in, she would ask to stand beside me. She did so and as the ship sailed past one soldier seemed to be waving more frantically than all the rest, and to him she waved back, quite clearly at this, her first sight of the man she was going to marry.

Many romances were started in the war by correspondence, a great number of them having their origin in the 'glory bags' that almost all South African women at some time or another sent to troops on active service. Made of khaki drill, the bags contained woollen socks, balaclavas, and other items to add some comfort to the austerity of life in the front lines, and it became a custom to include a good luck note. Lonely soldiers began corresponding with their unknown benefactors and it was from these, more often than not, self-conscious, 'thank-you' notes that friendships grew and in many cases culminated in marriage.

A romantic legend was at one stage even woven around me. It was started, I understand, by some sentimental British soldier who somehow believed that my sweetheart had run off to join the forces, and that I, lonely and broken-hearted, had taken to singing to every troopship that came into Durban in the hope that my erstwhile admirer would hear my voice and return to me.

Some Australian troops and I were unwittingly involved in an incident which brought down on my head the official wrath of South African governmental authorities in the form of a letter stating that my singing had caused damage to the extent of £70 to a harbour installation. When the *Felix Roussel* came into harbour packed with Australians, she was, in the technical language of seamen, very 'tender'. She was, in other words, heavily laden with troops and equipment, and, being extremely unwieldy, it was essential that the weight be evenly distributed as the harbour pilot, Captain George Lindsay, carefully manoeuvred her in very windy weather towards her place alongside the quay. The troops had been instructed to remain roughly in equal numbers on either side of the ship while this delicate operation was in progress and all was going well until, about 10 yards from the quay, my voice singing 'Waltzing Matilda' rang out. Instantly the troops on the far deck rushed to the side opposite the wharf and all Captain Lindsay's careful plans were in that second ruined. The ship gave a terrific list and in doing so her masts crashed into the overhead feed of the grain elevator, causing £70 damage.

Nothing further was heard of the incident – though it remained a favoured item in Captain Lindsay's repertoire of reminiscences – but I have often wondered how, in the stilted language of a Government department, the episode was explained away.

Among the entries in my autograph book is a signature, regrettably indecipherable, and one which I cannot recall to mind. It was put there by an Australian, a Lt.-commander in the Royal Australian Navy who wore the ribbon of the George Medal on his chest, but for what it was awarded to him I was never able to prise from him. He was a magnificent swimmer and a deep-sea diver, so one can only surmise that it was related in some way or another to those fields that the highest award for bravery – out of the front line – was awarded to him.

He was aboard one of the Australian naval vessels that from time to time visited Durban. The first ever to arrive was HMAS *Shropshire*, which in December 1940 escorted a convoy into Durban. Later a destroyer, the *Napier*, came in to leave two hospital cases behind and then, soon after the war's end, we saw the heavy cruiser HMAS *Australia*, which was one of the first targets in the war of Japan's 'kamikaze' pilots. The Australians, whose reputation for wild, uninhibited behaviour rests on the traditions established by their fathers in World War I, left an indelible impression on Durban's wartime memories. Port officials, police and others responsible for law and order would give an involuntary shudder when they heard that a convoy with Australians on board was expected, for they knew that, come what may, Durban was in for a boisterous spell which would end only when their ships rounded the harbour exit for the open sea.

I had a soft spot for the Australians, a sentiment that was warmly shared by another Durbanite, Ethel Campbell. Our friendship dated back to kindergarten days. She in the First World War was known as the 'Angel of Australia' for her kindness to Australian troops passing through to the European battlefields. We worked together in the West Street canteen in World War I – I had resisted Ethel

Campbell's exuberant suggestion the moment war was declared that we both become nurses – and I became involved in her enthusiasm for the Australians. When she heard that a shipload of Australians had been confined to their ship to prevent a recurrence of the exploits of a previous shipload of their countrymen who, once ashore, had painted the town red, she commandeered her father's horse and carriage and then loading it with cans of hot tea, tins of biscuits, and sacks of oranges, from the West Street canteen of which my mother was chairwoman, we set off for the docks. Ethel, whose ingenuity had not overlooked the problem of passing the gifts up to the soldiers in the ships, had brought with her a number of empty bottles and some string and with the help of these the tea and other items were hauled up by the soldiers on the decks.

In 1960, Sir Eric Harrison, the Australian High Commissioner in London, in the course of his speech at the Anzac Day celebration recalled his visit to Durban aboard a troopship in 1916 and mentioned that he had been at the receiving end of one of the oranges I had thrown up to the men on the deck.

The gratitude of the Australians in the early days of World War I so touched Ethel that from then on Australians became her special charge and she would be down at the docks where, always wearing a sailor collar, and having mastered the intricacies of semaphore, she would signal to incoming ships asking, 'Any Australians aboard?' If there were they were given preferential treatment by Ethel over the troops from all other lands. It was not surprising, therefore, that after the war the Australians, with war memories of her generosity, invited her to their country as the guest of the Ex-Servicemen's Association. She went with her father, Dr. Sam Campbell, and was given a royal reception wherever she went.

Poor health prevented her from extending in World War II her generous hospitality to Australians, but in her home in Hilton Road, Durban, where she lived with her widowed mother, Australians were always warmly welcomed guests. With memories of their antics in World War I, she used to listen with relish to their World War II escapades in Durban – picking up, bodily, 'baby' cars, with women drivers in them and depositing them on the pavement, or holding up a brewery truck and helping themselves to bottles of beer. When she died in 1933 a great character passed from the Durban scene.

New Zealanders, whom one automatically associated with the Australians, were, generally speaking, a more gentle race and were firm favourites of Durban. I sang frequently to ships carrying New Zealanders and, having made a study of the singing of Maori folk-songs, was able to provide them with vivid reminders of home. I discovered during the course of the war that I was distantly related to one of the most courageous soldiers New Zealand produced in World War II, Lt. Charles Upham, the double VC. He was captured in Tobruk. In Italian and German prisoner-or-war camps, New Zealand and South African troops were often incarcerated together, and at one time he was in the same room as my brother-in-law, Captain Guy Gibson, of the Durban Royal Light Infantry. In fact, Guy Gibson occupied the lower bunk of a double-decker bed, and Upham the top one. Upham's exploits are by now famous, including the one witnessed by so many Allied soldiers in the camp when Upham, announcing that he proposed leaving the camp, took a run and tried to jump and clamber over a 12 ft. double barbed-wire fence, ending up hopelessly ensnarled in the mesh. With the camp guards in an uproar, Upham philosophically pulled out his pipe awaiting the German sentries and his inevitable 'month in solitary'.

On another occasion, when German motor convoys were transporting Allied prisoners from Italy – then on the point of surrender – into Germany, Upham decided to make another escape attempt at the moment the convoy had slowed almost to walking pace as it made its way across the pontoon bridge that replaced the destroyed steel bridge over the River Po. Notwithstanding the fact that the convoy bristled with German guards armed with automatic rifles and machine guns, Upham leapt off and headed across the farmland with the Germans in pursuit, firing everything that could fire. Upham, it seemed, had a charmed life. Anyone else would almost certainly have been shot dead. Upham had the heel of his boot shot off and was recaptured hiding behind the trunk of a tree. The Germans, who had an immense respect for the ribbon of the Victoria Cross and Bar which Upham wore, regarded his exploits with tolerant amusement and he was pushed back into the truck.

Years later in London when Upham was there for the presentation ceremonies in Buckingham Palace, I met his sister, Mrs. Holmes Siedle, to whom, as I have said, we are distantly related.

It was a New Zealander and not an Australian, oddly enough, who wrote out for me all the words of 'Waltzing Matilda'. He was Sapper G. Jackson, of Christchurch, who also asked me to accept a Maori souvenir in appreciation of what my singing had meant to him. It proved to be a beautiful lucky greenstone with gold leaves, a memento I still treasure.

On 11 February 1944 I helped cement bonds of friendship with another of our Allies – the Poles, represented that day by a shipload of Polish women, 627 of them, who were being transferred from refugee camps in Karachi, Kenya, Tanganyika and Rhodesia, to Britain, where they were to join the Polish wing of the WAAF. I did not realize until the ship drew opposite me that there were not troops but women aboard and that they were in a pitiful state, physically and mentally. What clothes they had were in rags and their spirit was so low that they just did not react to my song of welcome.

What a transformation had taken place by the time those women resumed their journey to Britain! Through the energy and drive of the Major of the Natal WAAS (Women's Army Auxiliary Service), Hanise Pollack, the Polish women were taken to Clairwood Racecourse and soon were housed comfortably in converted stables; were having their morale restored by a small army of hairdressers whom Hansi Pollack rounded up; and were fitted out with women's army uniforms – a concession which Hansi Pollack wrung from Defence Headquarters by her eloquence in convincing the military powers-that-be that it would be a poor reflection on South Africa's reputation for hospitality to her Allies if the women were allowed to continue their journey in the ragged clothing in which they had arrived.

I was at the docks to sing a farewell to them when the *Ile de France*, which was to take them to Britain sailed. The women laughed and sang and called down to me for request songs.

I learned years later from a Royal Naval officer who had been stationed in Liverpool of the moving encounter that occurred just outside Liverpool between the *Ile de France* arriving with the Polish women on board and a ship that was sailing from Liverpool laden with Polish soldiers. The ships passed close to each other in the stream and there were tearful, happy greetings shouted in Polish as the two groups, so far removed from their brutally shattered homeland, recognized each other.

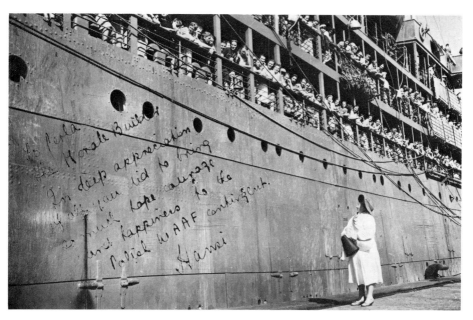

Her friend scribbled the compliments on the photograph, not – as it appears – on the side of the *Ile de France*!

Clad in Highland souvenir dress Perla waves to welcoming friends at the dockside at Durban after a post-war visit to the UK.

Perla at Forfar Scotland 1949.

— 12 —

The troops come home

They sounded the last 'All Clear' on 15 August 1945. The most terrible war in history was finally over after six years that had seemed like six decades. It would be a long time before a shattered civilization had pulled itself together and adapted to the new world yet to emerge from the carnage and destruction, but this day was for celebration and down at the docks there were joyous scenes. I went aboard a British destroyer; the first vessel I had set foot on since the start of the war, in terms of my determination to do nothing that could in any way possibly infringe any security regulation and thereby jeopardize my precious 'Dockside Entertainer's' pass.

I was at the docks at six that morning and made my first call on Captain Nicholas in the Port Captain's headquarters. He was as hard at work as ever, a berthing plan in front of him and a loudspeaker blaring out instructions to an incoming convoy. There was no time for expressions of our mutual happiness so I left him with a four-inch Union Jack which I planted firmly in the middle of his berthing plan and then hurried off to greet the convoy. I had a Union jack stuck jauntily in my red hat and when I reached my usual place I found that I was to enjoy the luxury of being accompanied . . . by a band. Lieut. Phillips had brought his SA Air Force band down to the docks and as they saw me approach they played 'Where Did You Get That Hat'. It was a joyous day in which the cheers of the returning troops, the shouts of happiness from the crowds of civilians waiting to welcome them home mingled with the pealing church bells as Durban gave thanks for peace.

I sang a welcome to the *Reina del Pacifico*, which came in packed with South African troops, and spent the remainder of that day sharing the happiness of peace with all the thousands of soldiers, sailors and civilians to whom the docks, for so many years, had symbolized the heartbreak of ships and men leaving for destinations from which so many would not return.

Only one ship, the *Samoa*, sailed that day and on the following day there was no movement of shipping at all. We celebrated.

But then began in earnest the mighty task of restoring the countless thousands of soldiers to their homelands and in the days which followed, the troopships started coming in bringing their joyous cargoes of men who would soon be back in 'civvy street'. On the morning that I sang goodbye to HMS *Howe*, with Viscount Curzon on board, I learned that the *Bergenfjord* was in the outer anchorage and had on board the No. 7 Wing of the No. 2 South African Air Force fighter squadron – my husband's old squadron. They had been shipped out of Italy for the Far East and had reached Colombo when Japan capitulated. The ship promptly turned round and came to South Africa.

This was really a sentimental reunion for me and I hurried home to fetch the Squadron flag which my husband had sent me from Egypt, after El Alamein, with the names of all the Squadron members inscribed on it. As the *Bergenfjord* sailed in I waved the flag as I sang and received, in return, ear-splitting cheers.

There was also increased activity on the part of the hospital ships at this time, bringing the wounded and ill back from hospitals scattered around the world and picking up those patients in South Africa that could now be repatriated to Britain. The difference now was that relatives and friends were allowed into the dock area to greet the patients as they came down the gangway. There were, of course, many moving and emotional moments of reunion, but the realization that we were at last seeing the final act of the great tragedy made these moments bearable. When the South African hospital ship *Cap St. Jacques* came in with so many nursing staff on board who were old friends of mine – the Matron, Estella Richard, Sisters Kathleen Dunn, Ella Rose Williams, and Marjorie Press among them . . . there was a moment of panic when the ship caught fire while in the dock. A major surgical operation had later to be performed on the ship – gaping holes cut into her side by means of oxy-acetyene torches – before she was ready for sea again.

One after the other the mighty ships bringing the troops home came sailing into Durban and provoked such scenes of wild enthusiasm among the huge crowds of civilians gathered to greet them that it was a miracle that many did not suffer serious injury. When the *Carnarvon Castle* came in in October with 5,000 soldiers on board the crowds broke down the barriers and it was all the guards could do to restrain them from rushing headlong over the quayside.

The sight of the huge crowds waiting at the docks to greet the returning ships soon became commonplace and it was, therefore, with some surprise that the minesweeper *Imrof* arrived virtually unnoticed. She deserved a welcome if ever a ship did. She had sailed from Alexandria but encountered almost continuous mechanical trouble throughout the entire voyage which took her three whole months to complete.

Without giving a moment's thought to the semantics of whether a flying boat rightly belonged to the realm of the sea or the air, I stood on the dockside on 31 October to sing a welcome to troops who returned home from the Middle East in a Sunderland flying boat of No. 35 Squadron, SAAF. It landed in Durban Bay and our canteen had been asked to provide the disembarking troops with refreshments from the mobile canteen. A Sunderland was named 'Little Lulu' and had an emblem painted on her fuselage showing Lulu holding a letter addressed to the Emperor of Japan. 'Little Lulu' never got round to delivering her 'letter', which would have been in the shape of a bomb, but had her services pressed instead into the mammoth task of helping to repatriate South African troops. It was an experimental flight on this occasion but proved so successful that the Sunderlands continued to operate an almost continuous shuttle-service until the repatriation operation had been completed.

After disembarking from the Sunderland the men were brought to the jetty by boat and were standing up in it, their faces eagerly scanning the crowds of people on the quayside. Those on shore were equally intent in their efforts to recognize a familiar face and the atmosphere, so unlike that which prevailed when the crowded troopships came in, was unaccountable tense. I gave a loud 'Cooee' and then began to sing 'It's a Hap-hap-happy Day' and within seconds the mood had changed and everyone on shore was singing a welcome with me.

The shuttle-service continued operating until March, and on one of the last flights there was a charming – and as far as I know never-before-told-incident involving General Everard Poole, who commanded the Sixth South African Division in Italy. One of the airmen on board had with him his squadron's pet dog which, contrary to all regulations, he had smuggled on board rather than leave it behind in Italy. As the Sunderland neared Durban the problem of the likely reaction of the military and civil authorities to the presence of the dog on board became a pressing one and in the general discussion, which now involved everyone, General Poole came up with a solution – one which only he, by reason of his high rank, could bring about. He had a brief talk with the aircraft's captain and then, taking the dog in his arms, he stood by the door and as the flying boat was slowly taxiing across the bay to its moorings the general slid the door open sufficiently far to allow him to drop the dog gently into the water. It promptly swam ashore, shook itself and was waiting for its master who, like everyone else on the aircraft including General Poole, self-consciously gave the impression that they hadn't the faintest idea why a dog should be on the quayside wagging its tail and yelping with delight at seeing them.

Work continued apace dismantling the facades of war that had for so long enshrouded the docks and many familiar naval and military establishments that I had known so well were closing down. Even the Seamen's Institute reverted, in time, to its civilian status and carried on serving merchant seamen.

On the first Remembrance Day of peace – 11 November, which fell on a Sunday – we gathered in Durban's City Hall to pay homage to the dead of two world wars. I was on the platform with the Durban Civic Orchestra, under the baton of Edward Dunn, and led the big crowd that was present in the singing of hymns of remembrance and thanksgiving.

The Royal Naval Auxiliary Hospital at Wentworth, where I had spent so many Friday afternoons singing to the patients in the wards, received orders in December to close down and on learning this from Rear-Admiral G.V. Hobbs, in charge of the hospital, I invited all those patients physically able to do so, to visit Pineholme for a last farewell get-together.

More than 4,200 patients passed through Wentworth in the war years, some of them never having risen from their beds from the time of their arrival until their departure. On the day they were taken down to the docks to board the hospital ship *Tjitjalengka*, the kind-hearted drivers of the ambulances made quick, circular tours of Durban to give the men a glimpse of the city which they had never seen though they had been in it for so long. It was pouring with rain the day the ship sailed and the patients had to be carried aboard with groundsheets and oilskins covering them.

One patient who was both the 'oldest inhabitant' of Wentworth and one of the most popular, was Leading Stoker S.R. 'Winnie' Winson, who had sailed in HMS *Cumberland*, escorting the convoys to Russia, but had contracted spinal tuberculosis and spent the remainder of the war years in Durban. He was in high spirits when he, and his pet budgie, left in the hospital ship. When he arrived in England he wrote me a letter in which he compared the send-off the ship had been given, with me standing singing on the dockside, and the reception accorded it on its arrival in Britain. 'Just two solitary, blue-nosed policemen waiting on the quayside', he wrote.

It took many months to repatriate all the troops and the beginning of the new year still saw ships coming into Durban laden with soldiers. There was a strange encounter in the docks one day in January which brought home forcibly to me the senseless irony of war. On board the *Stratheden* were 3,000 South Africans returning from Italy. Watching them arrive were 3,000 Italians who had been prisoners of war and who were due to sail in the *Malorca* to their homes in Italy. The victorious and the vanquished gazed at each other but there was no animosity now. Both sides were going home. The hatred fomented by war had been dissipated and the docks resounded to laughter and cheering. The final unrealistic touch to the scene was added by there being aboard the South African troopship a number of Italian women, the brides of South African soldiers stationed in Italy.

It was just at this time that the BBC devoted a programme to the 'Lady in White'. It was by John Whitehouse, who had first-hand knowledge, having been in the aircraft carrier *Illustrious*, which visited Durban in wartime, and where he met me on several occasions. The programme brought in its wake numbers of letters from people throughout Britain and I was later to hear from John Whitehouse that he, too, had received letters from pleased listeners. One of them from Mrs. E. Still of Bloomsbury Lane, Timperley, Cheshire, said: 'Thank you, John Whitehouse, for the most beautiful and human talk I have heard on the wireless. My boy was one who passed through Durban.'

Inured though we had become to the horrors of war we were still shocked when told of the experiences endured by some of those imprisoned by the Japanese. There was, for example, Mrs. Brunhile Zwankhuysen, who had been interned for four years in Java. She came into Durban on board the liner *Antenor* in March and we learned from her some details of the horrors she had survived. On one occasion she and four other women in the camp were caught eating some eggs they had found and were sentenced to be hanged. Fortunately for Mrs Zwankhuysen she found that she was just able to rest her toes on the ground and in this way was able to support her weight. This, at best, was a temporary expedient and she faced the certainty of death by slow strangulation when her saviour – in the person of a visiting Japanese general – appeared on the scene. He demanded to know why the five women were being hanged and on hearing the trivial reason ordered them to be cut down. Mrs. Zwankhuysen was the only one to survive the ordeal. When we met her in Durban the marks left by the rope were still clearly visible on her neck.

There was an endless stream of horror stories flowing from the Far East almost from the very start of the war against Japan until long after VJ Day. Theses were, however, from time to time lightened by episodes of great happiness – vignettes played against the background of Durban as the cross-roads of the wartime world.

A mother with two little girls with her was on board a ship which was torpedoed and in the confusion as the ship went down she lost one of her daughters. She arrived broken-hearted in Durban with only the one child. Soon after arriving the child took ill and was taken to the Durban Children's Hospital. The mother went to visit the child and as she was walking through the wards she saw her other daughter lying in a cot. By some miracle the baby girl had survived the sinking and had been brought to Durban.

Another amazing coincidence was of a woman who had been evacuated from the Far East. Her husband, she had convincing reasons for believing, had been killed. One day she went into the foreign exchange department of a Durban bank to exchange some money. She gave her name and the bank clerk said 'That's strange. You're the second person from the Far East with that name whom I have attended to this morning.' The other 'person' was her husband, who had reached Durban believing she was dead.

As the months of the new year of peace slipped by honours were bestowed on the men and women who, in the eyes of their grateful countries, had rendered services which deserved recognition. It was with a sense of deep pride that I, on 7 March, learned that I was to receive the King's commendation for my war services. Three other South Africans were similarly honoured. There was Mr. E. Stephan of Cape Town who for four years had listened in night after night to broadcasts from Berlin, Tokyo, Singapore, Rome and Java giving details of Allied prisoners of war. In the course of the war he succeeded in tracing thousands of prisoners and communicated their whereabouts to their relatives.

Mrs. I. Sanderson, also of Cape Town, received her commendation for being 'Ma' to South African prisoners in Italy and Germany to whom she wrote more than 3,000 letters. The fourth recipient was Mr. O.J. Sibbett of Cape Town, who founded the national thrift movement in South Africa.

As gratifying as the award itself of the Certificate of Commendation from the King, was the reaction of Durban and its citizens. Durban bestowed on me the highest civic honour it was empowered to do and I received scores of telegrams and letters, typical of which was one written by Mr. A.W.J. Johnson:

'There must be thousands all over the world who will rejoice with us all in South Africa in the news that Mrs. Perla Siedle Gibson has been commended by the King.

'How many thousands must remember the "Lady in White" as they glided away from the docks. They will never forget her. Many have gone to the Great Beyond, yet they crowd around me as I write, sending tidings of great joy and pleasure. Our soldiers will never forget what that voice meant to them as they were torn from their loved ones at the dock gate. She bridged their sorrow with her voice.

'Her voice was the last link for some of these brave lads before vanishing from these shores. How she must have softened the blow that was to come to them.

'Her voice uttered the unspoken thoughts and hopes of their loved ones wherever they may have been and who, with heavy hearts could utter no sound of joy.

'To many of us she is a sacred memory – a human voice used for good and noble ends. We will never forget her.'

The *Natal Daily News*, at this same time, made these comments:

'Even though from the first song the gratitude of the departing men must have provided its own stimulus and reward, it cannot have been easy for Madame Perla Siedle Gibson to have persisted.

'We are a shy and rather stiff-necked people, more afraid of being emotionally expressive or sentimental than of the bombs of the enemy. Would other people deride it? Would one be charged with vanity or with making oneself foolish? Perhaps the fact that Madame Perla Siedle is also a wife and a mother whose own men were serving braced her against pettiness of thought once she could see an obvious need and do something about it.

'Letter not only to the Lady in White but to others bear tribute to the warmth, the touch of humanity and the comfort her singing often brought. Men and women felt suddenly less lonely. They were reminded that despite the formality, the discipline and the insignificance that numbers always impose on an individual, they were persons playing their part in a noble cause. They are reminded of precious human values. Did the Lady White not also give utterance to the feelings of hundreds of us who were not able, or were too shy to find expression for them. Durban might well think it over and perhaps devise some means of paying its own tribute to one who has brought honour to her city even as she has earned it for herself.'

Soon afterwards I learned of the unanimous decision of the Durban City Council to honour me civically. The official citation read:

'On behalf of the people of this city, the Durban City Council this day paid honour to

PERLA SIEDLE GIBSON

in recognition of the great services rendered by her to this city and the cause of this country and its allies during the Second World War, which won for her the proud and affectionate title of "The Lady in White", by which she is so widely known both here and in other parts of the world.'

Another honour fell to our family soon afterwards.

My husband Jack – Sergeant C.W. Gibson, BEM – was picked to go with the Springbok contingent to London for the Victory Parade. They were, originally, to have gone by ship, but there was at that time such a demand for shipping space that it was decided to fly the contingent of 250 in South African Air Force Dakotas. There was a march past before they left – the most highly decorated body of men ever to march through Durban. There was one VC, one DSC, nine DSOs, 12 MCs, 13 DFCs, 50 MMs, 17 BEMS, and a sprinkling of AFMs, MBEs, DSMs, and DCMs.

At General Poole's request I sang a farewell to the contingent as they boarded the Dakotas – fourteen of which took off in two flights. My husband Jack had reason to believe on that memorable visit to London when the world thrilled to the magnificent pageantry of the troops of the Empire saluting their King, that the number 13 had a special significance for him. The Dakota in which he flew was No. 13; it had mechanical trouble on Military Airfield No. 13 – Nairobi; and the mechanics' repair kit was labelled 13. He failed, however, to capitalize on this sequence of 13s when, on arrival in Britain, he found that Derby was being run on the 13th and the winner was destined to be a horse No. 13.

I sang frequently to ships coming and going in those busy months after VJ Day when the world was re-establishing itself on to a normal peace-time basis. On Christmas night, in the midst of a happy family gathering at Pineholme, I received a message that a very special ship was due to dock and would I be there to greet her. It was the *Maloja*, the last troopship to return from Europe, bringing with it the South African unit which had staffed the repatriation camp in Genoa. On board, too, were many former British ex-servicemen who were coming to settle in South Africa.

But joy, as always, is blended with sadness. In this year my father died, aged 92. He left a heritage that is for ever imprinted on almost every facet of Durban public life. The part he played in the growth of the shipping industry and the development of Durban's harbour is enshrined by the gracious gesture of the South African Government in naming one of the most powerful harbour tugs after him – the *Otto Siedle*. In almost every field of welfare work his name, with that of my mother, occupies an honoured place, and the arts, culture and sport all acknowledge their deep debt of gratitude to him for his untiring and selfless devotion to their causes. Industry, too, remembers Otto Siedle. He pioneered many enterprises that today are among the economic mainstays of Natal – including the coal and glass industries.

—— 13 ——

Royal gratitude

Symbol of the British Empire's unity and steadfastness of purpose in the war was the King and his family and it was, with a deep sense of pride, that in March 1947 I was formally presented to the Queen at a tea-party at the City Hall on the morning of the Royal Family's arrival in Durban. Huge crowds thronged the gardens around the City Hall as the guests who had been invited to the reception entered the City Hall. My husband Jack and I took our places on one of the balconies overlooking the gardens and no sooner had we done so than someone in the crowd spotted me and called on me to sing to them while awaiting the arrival of the royal party. I led them in community singing until the cavalcade bringing the royal guests came into view and soon afterwards we all moved into the beautifully flower-bedecked City Hall, where the civic reception was being held.

It was a gay animated scene that was dominated by the personality and charm of the King and his family. In the midst of it all the Mayoress of Durban, Mrs. Clare Ellis Brown, came over and said: 'The Queen would like to speak to you, Perla.' The only thought that flashed through my mind at that instant was one of horror that one of the gloves I was wearing had split as I was applauding, but this was no time for sartorial niceties and, following the Mayoress, I found myself seated between the Queen and the two Princesses.

The Queen was charming. She said to me: 'We have heard a great deal about you and your singing and what a

wonderful help it has been to our men. We thank you.'
I replied that it had been a great privilege, one that I would
not have forgone for anything. In answer to her questions I
told of how I had first come to sing at the docks and then,
encouraged by her obvious interest went on to tell of my
husband Jack taking part in London's Victory Parade,
adding: 'He has never stopped talking about England's
hospitality – the celebrations and the stars which shone, on
that day, from your beautiful eyes.' She smiled and added:
'How charming of him to say that.'

At the end of the civic reception, as the Royal party
moved down the aisle towards the exit, the Queen paused at
our table to bow to Jack.

I was again to have the opportunity of being presented to
the King and Queen – this time at the Royal Garden Party
that Durban held the next day in honour of the royal visitors.
The King, bronzed and well-looking, said to me after I had
been formally presented to him: 'I have heard so much of
your work for my people in the war and I want to thank you
for the great help you gave them.' And then, with that keen
intelligence which caused him to take a deep personal
interest in anything which caught his imagination, he
inquired what kind of songs I sang and which vantage point
on the docks I used as a platform. With Princess Elizabeth
standing alongside him I recalled details of my dockside
singing days and drew a laugh from both of them when I
told how, as the ships drew near, the soldiers yelled 'Hullo
Ma', and the temptation I had to repress a retort that I felt a
little too much emphasis was being placed on the 'Ma'!

The preparations for the royal visit to Durban provided a
period of great excitement and expectation, heightened for
me by receiving a request from the BBC to take part in the
broadcast programme 'This is Africa – historical
background'. The interview included my singing a song of

CLARENCE HOUSE
S.W. 1

29th December, 1966

Dear Mrs. Gibson,

Queen Elizabeth The Queen Mother bids me tell
you how touched she was to receive your kind message of
good wishes for her speedy recovery.

Her Majesty is graciously pleased to accept the
book you sent her, and I am to say how well she remembers
all you did to cheer troops during the war by singing to
them, and that you sang to Their Majesties when they
arrived in South Africa in 1947.

I am to send you Queen Elizabeth's thanks, and
good wishes for 1967.

Yours sincerely,

Lady-in-Waiting

A Royal missive

With HRH Princess Alice, South Africa House, London, 1963.

With Lord Louis Mountbatten before the start of the Burma Star celebrations in Royal Albert Hall in May 1964.

welcome to which I wrote both words and music.

The Royal Family had journeyed to South Africa in HMS *Vanguard* and when that most majestic of all British battleships steamed into Durban harbour – the Royal Family had already visited Natal travelling overland – I was at the docks to sing a song of welcome in accordance with my wartime undertaking that I would always sing to ships of the Royal Navy. Her massive, magnificent pearl grey outline was silhouetted against a rainy sky as she sailed through the harbour entrance, and, as she drew near I gave a loud 'Cooee' and then sang 'Rule Britannia' and 'Land of Hope and Glory', followed by 'Sarie Marais'. There was a moment of silence as the last note faded away and then every craft in the harbour seemed to go mad as sirens, hooters and ships whistles rent the air in welcome. As the *Vanguard* was being berthed I was on the quayside singing old war songs to the delighted sailors, some of whom had passed through Durban during the war and remembered me. One of these was Engineer Commander Beale who, at a ball given on board the battleship, came up to me and recalled that he had heard me singing when he was in HMS *Exeter* – later sunk by the Japanese.

I sang farewell to the *Vanguard* when she left and then returned home to find a note awaiting from Lady Peel to say that the Queen wished to thank me for the words of my 'Song of Welcome', which had been printed on vellum and presented to her.

My next meeting with the Royal Family took place in 1952, but by then King George's untimely death had occurred.

His death was all the more saddening to us in Durban for preparations were well advanced for the King to recuperate in the Prime Minister's residence on the Natal south coast.

And I was to have had a special part to play in welcoming

the ailing King. I had received a telephone call from Scotland to ask me to sing 'Loch Lomond' as the *Vanguard* sailed into Durban, as a token of loyalty to the King by his Scottish subjects.

I was able that same year to convey personally to Queen Elizabeth my sorrow at her father's death. In London I was present at the annual commemoration service of the Knights of St Michael and St. George in St. Paul's Cathedral when the Earl and Countess of Clarendon – he had years earlier been South Africa's Governor-General – saw me and invited me to Ambassador's Court in St. James' Palace, his official residence as the Queen's Lord Chamberlain.

My daughter Joy and I visited them and found their interest in South Africa undiminished, with Lady Clarendon being particularly interested in the progress of the Children's Hospital in Durban which my mother had been instrumental in founding. Mention was made of the Royal Garden Party to be held in Buckingham Palace, and Lord Clarendon said that we – Joy, her husband Howard, and I should be presented. On my inquiring how one went about arranging an invitation to attend, Lord Clarendon said with a twinkle, 'It's simple. You just write to the Lord Chamberlain.' I went one better than that. I persuaded him to draft the letter I should formally write to him. This he promptly did and off we went in the certainty that, armed as we were with a letter to the Lord Chanberlain, drafted by none other than the Lord Chamberlain himself, there could be no doubt about the correctness of our approach. In due course the invitations arrived and we went to the Palace. Lord Clarendon was with the Queen and nodded to us to approach when he saw us. We curtsied and the Queen, lovely and gracious and far too young, I felt, to bear the awful responsibility of her high office, said she remembered us from Durban. 'Do you still sing to the ships?' she asked.

I told her I did and added: 'We were all very sad at hearing the news of the death of your father, the King.'

When I told the Queen that I was in London for the wedding of my daughter her face lit up and she said: 'Oh, I would so like to meet her.' So Joy, too, was presented.

I was to meet the Queen on yet another occasion. This was in 1955 when the Queen and the Duke of Edinburgh received the members of the BCESL War Graves pilgrimage from Durban in Buckingham Palace.

'Oh, but we have met before', said the Queen. I then asked after the Queen Mother, mentioning that Durban had completely lost its heart to the Royal Family on the occasion of their visit. The Queen replied: 'I shall be seeing her this afternoon and will give her your message.'

International politics took its inexorable course and within a few years South Africa ceased to be a member of the Commonwealth, a decision which was received with the deepest regret by a great many South Africans, particularly those in Natal, where the bonds of unity with the Royal Family were probably the strongest. But while political ties were severed the sentimental links will for ever be enshrined in the memories of those to whom the Queen and her family symbolize the historical greatness of Great Britain in peace and war.

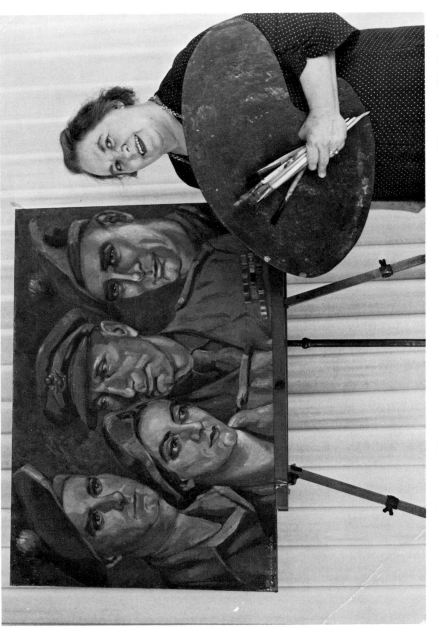

Perla Siedle Gibson – 'The Lady in White' – with a family portrait she painted during the war years. Sittings were fitted in when members of the family came home on leave. Left to right: Barrie, Joy, Jack Gibson, husband, and Roy who died of wounds in Italy.

— 14 —

Reunion

Security in wartime was so deeply an ingrained part of my being that I had no difficulty at all in falling in with the post-war 'secret machinations' of the BBC. I had received, in 1954, a message as mysterious as it was unexpected from Mr. Larry Forrester, Special Investigator of the 'Ask Pickles' television programme, asking if I would be prepared to make a special trip to London and, if so, to undertake it without divulging the fact to anyone. The 'Ask Pickles' show is one which attempts to gratify the requests of viewers who nominate particular happenings or incidents they would like to see re-enacted and thousands of requests had apparently poured in from World War II soldiers and their families asking if my dockside singing episodes could be re-created. In the letter I received Mr. Forrester said that the majority of requests had been for 'two loved ladies – Miss Gracie Fields and yourself – the Lady in White'. His letter continued: 'I would like you to see some of these letters. They are mostly from ex-servicemen who heard you during the war and they still keep the memory of your singing fresh in their hearts after ten years and more.

'Many have written to say that they have told their wives and children about you and that their families want to hear you as well.'

It was all triggered off, I was to learn, from an exchange of letters that appeared in the Live Letters column of the London *Daily Mirror*. Ex-Chief Petty Officer E.F. Sturgess of Carshalton, Surrey, wrote to the newspaper asking who was the Lady-in-White so many millions of troops had been sung to during the war, adding that she met the troopships at any time of the day, regardless of the weather. 'I feel many ex-servicemen will remember her with gratitude', he added. I happened to see the letter in an overseas edition of the *Daily Mirror* and I replied to it, reciprocating the greetings, and giving the assurance that I was still alive and singing.

It was this, as I say, that prompted the BBC to write to me, and while my security measures were foolproof the BBC's, it seems, were not. A London newspaper managed to ferret out the fact that I had been invited to London for the programme and while I steadfastly maintained, in answer to inquiries from Durban newspapermen, following up the London report, that I knew nothing whatever about the matter the leakage had spoiled the surprise aspect which was the cardinal point of the whole show. The matter, thus, fell into abeyance and I had practically forgotten the whole episode when, about a year later, as I was about to leave to sing to a party of veterans of the Boer War, I had a telephone call from the BBC in London. The show was on again. Would I come, bringing with me my old white dress, my red hat and my megaphone – keep the whole thing secret.

I said I would, not giving a thought to the hectic rush to which I had committed myself when I said I would be in London on time. But somehow I managed it and was met at London airport under conditions of great secrecy by an individual who was described as the 'security officer' for the programme. Soon afterwards I was at work rehearsing for my television appearance. Timing, of course, was the first essential and, as it had to be co-ordinated with a full orchestra, it was a long and exhausting business. My appearance was to coincide with a special El Alamein programme and I was told that among the 8,000,000 viewers who normally looked at the programme there would be thousands of veterans who had passed through Durban in wartime.

Came the great moment and I, to my astonishment, found myself trembling with nervousness while waiting for my cue. The television theatre in which I was to appear was in total darkness, I could hear the soft mellifluous voice of Wilfrid Pickles sketching, in words, the scene at Durban docks in wartime, of my standing there awaiting the arrival of a convoy. . . . Then, from the violinist, crouched beside me in the darkness came the ping that gave me my note and my cue. I burst into 'Land of Hope and Glory' as the theatre was flooded with light and stood there – in my white dress and my red hat, the megaphone raised to my lips – an exact replica of those dockside scenes of nearly a generation before. The secrecy this time had been fool-proof and the audience in the theatre, composed at the special request of the War Office, of ex-soldiers who had passed through Durban, stared in momentary, silent, disbelief at this sudden materialization of memories they all shared and then rose to their feet and cheered and cheered.

It was a thrilling, moving experience that recalled for me, as well, those amazing dockside days. For the millions of viewers the picture they saw in their screens, I was told later, was a remarkably detailed and accurate representation of Durban docks with, as it appeared, my walking up and singing directly at them just as if they were troops on board a ship.

Wilfrid Pickles was delighted. He told me he had never before achieved such an effect. 'You had them all in tears', he kept saying. 'But it must be wonderful for you to know that you brought happiness tonight into more than 8,000,000 homes.'

I was besieged by ex-servicemen in my dressing room after the show and as I left the theatre in a mad rush to reach the El Alamein celebrations in the Wembley Stadium in time my way was blocked by a big crowd which sang 'For She's a Jolly

Good Fellow'. When, eventually, I did reach the Stadium the remembrance celebrations were over but I had lots to compensate, in the days ahead, for that disappointment.

Letters poured in from people who had seen the television programme and invitations reached me from all over Britain to attend functions and parties. One letter, typical of many I received, was from Mr J. Redfern of Chard, Somerset, who wrote:

> 'After seeing you on TV tonight memories came flooding back to me, although I still do not know your name.' (The envelope had been addressed simply The Lady in White care of the BBC, London.) 'I still remember your standing on the quay to welcome the convoy into what still seems to me the most beautiful place I have ever seen – Durban. We all spoke of you for years after leaving Durban.'

From Mr. and Mrs. Sharman, whose son had served in the RAF but had just recently died, I received a letter telling me of how their son had frequently spoken of me and the effect my singing had on him and his comrades. He had described his impressions of me in a letter on one occasion and now his parents, compiling a record of their son's life and writings, were anxious to meet and talk with me. This we arranged.

The most touching letter I received as a direct result of my television appearance came to me also addressed 'The Lady in White, care of Wilfrid Pickles, BBC, London.' It was from Mr. James P. Redman, a former captain in the Royal Artillery, who wrote:

> 'I, for one, am in no way ashamed to say that the tears rolled silently down my cheeks, and a lump came up in

my throat last night as I sat in front of the fire with my wife and daughter safe and sound with me, and watched you on television.

'Oh, what memories came flooding back. And how thankful we have been to God that we could sit in front of our fire. Many, many of my former comrades could not do so – but I am sure they, too were with you in spirit wherever they might be.

'You took our thoughts so deeply, too, to our son who is now a 2nd Lieutenant in the 23 (K) Battalion of the King's African Rifles and who, while you were singing 'Land of Hope and Glory' last night was probably on his back in his "nyumba" in the pouring rain somewhere in Kenya.

'He is going out on patrols every day after the Mau Mau for there are still places in the world where war is being waged. He, however, flew out direct to Nairobi and did not have the great inspiration and courage which you inspired in the heart of his father in Durban in 1941.

'It is very difficult for me to think how to say "Thank you" adequately and suitably for what you did for us. Perhaps your true reward is in the knowledge that you are still close and dear in the hearts of many hundreds of us – after all these years. But, humbly, I enclose a crest of the Royal Artillery which I have had for so many, many years and which travelled with me wherever we went – truly was it the motto "Ubique" in those days. Please be good enough to accept it in the spirit in which it is given and God bless you.'

On the crest was written: "To the Lady in White – in deepest gratitude for the inspiration she brought to our hearts in 1941 and for the tears she brought to our eyes in 1955.'

Mr. W.S. Loxton expressed his thoughts in verse, heading it 'Lady of Durban'.

> 'Crowded troopship; stinking night,
> Tropic stars ashining bright.
> Crown and anchor takes your cash,
> Prickly heat, itching rash.
> Your old private life is gone,
> Just a number you've become.
> Wondering what life's all about,
> Wondering what will put you out.
> Tropic diseases or Iti gun,
> Dying before your life's begun,
> Dreaming of the home you've left,
> Of mother, sweetheart, sad – bereft.
> Then suddenly out of Durban's pier
> Something white, dazzling, clear,
> A woman's voice just cries "Cooee",
> Loving soft, warm sympathy.
> Then from the megaphone's brass wrought mouth,
> Comes the song of eternal youth.
> "Land of Hope and Glory" sings,
> Dream of man. Dream of Kings.
> Just a woman's voice in the night,
> Just a girl dressed in white.
> Come to cheer us on our way,
> A glimpse of home at end of day.'

I had another memorable experience on that visit to Britain arising from its being remembrance week during which a party of South Africans was to make a pilgrimage to the war graves. I had actually sung a farewell to the party before it left Durban by ship and then, caught up by the unexpected

BBC developments, I found myself in London before the party arrived. After a flurry of telephone calls between London and Paris where Major Vaughan was in charge of all the arrangements for the pilgrimage to the war graves, I was asked to go to Dover to greet the Channel boat which was bringing the South African party from France to Britain.

The astonishment of the South Africans on board had to be seen to be believed. I had sung farewell to them in Durban and here I was again, in the flesh, on the quayside of Dover, welcoming them to Britain. What a reunion we had!

They were crowded days – days filled with reminders of personal tragedies that two world wars had been inflicted on my own small family circle. With Sir Ian Fraser, the blind MP, afterwards Lord Fraser, who was Chairman of St. Dunstan's, I attended the Albert Hall Festival of Remembrance and then, the following day, with Sir Ian at my side, planted two crosses in the Gardens of Remembrance – one in the plot of the Black Watch for my son, Roy, and the other in the section commemorating the Royal Heavy Artillery, for my brother, Karl.

The secrecy with which the BBC cloaked my arrival in Britain apparently proved infectious for I received a message from Tony Parker of Scunthorpe, Lincs, who had served in HMS *Nereide*, a frequent wartime visitor to Durban with Tony many times a guest at Pineholme. I was asked to attend the third birthday party of the Scunthorpe Naval Association but was told to keep it quiet as my unexpected appearance there at which I was to be nominated as an honorary life member of the Royal Naval Association would enable the local branch to score over their rivals, the Naval Association of the adjoining town of Doncaster. Again security stood the test and I was given a wonderful reception by 800 members of the Association who in wartime had passed through Durban. Then, with a bouquet of white chrysanthemums in my arms the honorary life membership badge was pinned on me and from then on the meeting dissolved into a rollicking sing-song in which all the old nostalgic tunes of Durban dockside days were sung.

Sir Ian Fraser had taken me under his protective wing and through his efforts I toured all the famous institutions for disabled ex-servicemen – St. Dunstan's, Lord Roberts' Workshops and the Star and Garter Home that stands in the very heart of England on top of Richmond Hill and cares for men who are almost totally disabled but who, nevertheless, continue living as normally as they can, working at hobbies and carrying on cheerfully and uncomplainingly.

When in 1959 I again visited Britain, having toured, with 400 other members of the British Commonwealth Ex-Service League, the British war cemeteries in Europe in which so many South Africans lie buried, we were the guests of Lord Louis Mountbatten, Grand President of the BCESL, who, somewhat to my surprise, knew all about my 'secret' visit to Scunthorpe and my being made an honorary life member of the Royal Naval Association. Lord Louis had seen the incident on television at the time and he asked me if I would be photographed alongside him standing in the gateway to his lovely home, Romsey.

Later that year I attended a gathering of the British Limbless Ex-Servicemen's League (Southern Area) as the guest of the chairman, Mr. Leonard Coles, and again – it was becoming almost a habit – I arrived, by pre-arranged plan, unannounced. The chairman told the big gathering of men in wheel-chairs, on crutches, others with artificial limbs and with empty sleeves, that he had a special surprise for them. I stepped from behind the curtain and the reception I received was overwhelming. After singing to them the men crowded around me, recalling the days when they had visited Durban – the vast majority as patients aboard hospital ships. Many said that they had never seen me in the flesh, but had heard my voice coming in through the portholes as they lay in bed unable to move.

I was also a guest at a ceremony at which wreaths were laid at the Cenotaph by the Burma Star Association, the salute being taken by Brigadier Sir John Smyth, VC, MC, MP. I had been asked to wear the medals won by my husband and my son, Roy – fourteen in all – and I did so, walking beside Sir John as he inspected the veterans lined up on the Horse Guards Parade. Some of the men shook hands with me and when the parade was over someone in the ranks shouted, 'Three cheers for the Lady-in-White'.

One of the officers I met that day was Major van Niekerk of the London Scottish and I inquired how he, bearing so well-known a South African name, gave every appearance in his manner and accent of being English. He told me that after his great-grandfather had been blinded in the Zulu wars the family had emigrated to England and had remained there ever since.

The Burma Star Association, not to be outdone, decided that they, too, must stage a reunion at which I would provide a nostalgic reminder of Durban in wartime and once again I found myself behind closed doors engaged in planning another hush-hush appearance. This time it was to be in the Albert Hall and the preparations for it were superbly organized. The Albert Hall was in complete darkness. I stood in the wings, in my white dress, red hat and with my megaphone, awaiting the cue that came as a carefully modulated voice described a ship, packed with men, approaching Durban harbour and then added 'As you entered Durban harbour you heard. . .'.

From the wings I gave the loud and familiar 'Cooee'. Then I strode on to the stage as all the spotlights focused on me, and 9,000 Burma Star veterans, electrified by the dramatic reconstruction of the scene they remembered so well, stood and cheered. It was a thrilling moment. Behind me was the band of the Coldstream Guards under the baton of Lieut.-Colonel Douglas A. Pope and to their accompaniment, as well as that contributed by Reg Kemish at the grand organ, I sang all the old songs.

I was received with immense kindness and friendship by everyone, including the guest of honour of that night, Field-Marshal Viscount Slim, who, with his staff at a private reception to which I had been invited, told me that he well remembered my singing when he was in Durban in the war and later, when he was returning to Britain in the *Jason* after completing his term of office as Governor-General of Australia.

The Australians were not to be left out of the act and later I was invited to attend reunions of the Australian Ex-Servicemen's Association and the Anzac Fellowship. Seated between Lord Birdwood of Anzac and the chairman, Mr. Nicholson, I proposed the toast of the Association, to which Viscount Bruce of Melbourne responded.

It seemed incredible that with the most terrible of all wars over, peace should still elude mankind and it was with a sense of deep sadness that I responded to the call to sing farewell in Durban in 1950 to a ship that was taking South African airmen to fight for the United Nations in Korea. Learning it was the Cheetah Squadron which would represent South Africa in the fighting, I took with me to the docks the squadron's flag which previously I had used to welcome the squadron when it returned home from the war. The airmen cheered and shouted when they saw the flag and enthusiastically joined me in singing – a complete flashback for me to the war years. On that day a mother of one of the airmen came up to me and said, 'Seeing you here

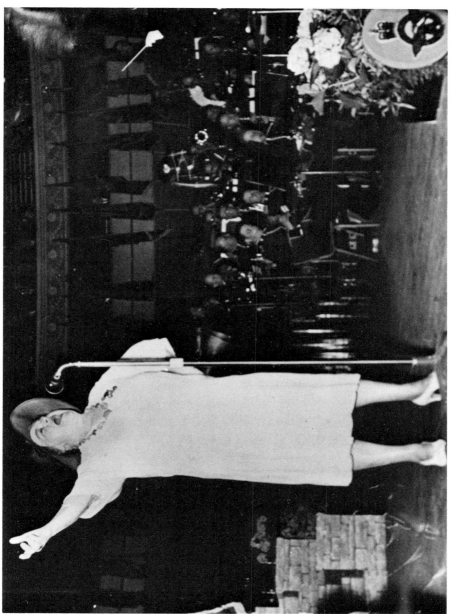

At the Burma Star Reunion Albert Hall 1959 and –

– the following morning inspecting Burma Star veterans with Brigadier Sir John Smyth VC, MC, MP, and wearing with pride the campaign medals and honours won by her husband and two sons.

singing good-bye to the lads makes it easier to endure. It seems only yesterday that my son came back from the war and now he's going again. But he told me you're his good luck charm – that if you sing to a ship nothing will happen to it. I am certain now he will come back safely.'

The Suez crisis cast its threatening shadow over the world only a few years after Korea had been eliminated as a danger to peace, and again I found myself singing to naval vessels and troopships that, unable to use the Suez Canal, resorted to the Cape route and called in at Durban.

Somewhat to my astonishment I received many letters at the time of the Suez crisis from families in England telling me that their sons or brothers or sweethearts were sailing for the Middle East via Durban and asking me to sing to them as I had done to their fathers in Word War II. It was a touching reminder of past associations.

Among the ships I sang to at this time was HMS *Narvik*, which was carrying an atomic bomb to Australia for testing. Several troopships, among them the *Nevassa* and the *Empire Orwell*, taking soldiers back to Britain after their tours of duty in the Far East, called at Durban and I was there to welcome them. The scenes that I remembered so well from the war days were repeated and, but for the fact that no security measures were enforced at the docks and that the troopships were infinitely more comfortable and roomier than those of World War II days, with consequently less tension among the men aboard them, I would have found it difficult to realize that the transition from war to peace had, in fact, taken place. The same sentimentality prevailed among the troops and I was particularly touched by two incidents which occurred. The first was in June 1957 when, prevented by a bout of 'flu from being at the docks to welcome the *Empire Orwell*, I received a radio message from the officer commanding the troops reading, 'All much regret your indisposition. You were greatly missed. All troops send good wishes.'

The other was when the *Oxfordshire* came into Durban on 30 April – my birthday – and I, to my astonishment as I stood on the docks, saw a huge banner strung out, reading 'Happy birthday to the Lady-in-White'. How they knew it was my birthday I shall never know, but for me it was the most moving and rewarding 'present' I think I have ever received to be standing there and listening to the soldiers singing 'Happy Birthday To You' and 'Why Was She Born So Beautiful'. I was escorted aboard the *Oxfordshire*, soon after it had docked, and on the top-deck encircled by cheering troops, was a huge birthday cake. Speeches were made by the ship's captain and by the OC troops and – for me – a memorable birthday ended with our singing the old songs together.

—— 15 ——

Full Circle

To us you were the mother of all men as you sang us on our way.'

The speaker was a kilted highlander. The year – 1963. It sent my thoughts spinning back more than two decades to that day on Durban docks when I had looked up in response to the shouts of 'Hey, Ma! What about a song, Ma?' – the cries that set me on the broad path of duty I was destined to follow; gathering as I went friendship of thousands of men and women around the world, the rich, the famous, the humble, the poor, each of whom in his own peculiar way had derived some little comfort, a brief moment of reassurance, from hearing my voice on that wartime dockside.

I am still treading that same path. I realized that as I stood listening to that highlander – a generation older now, his face lined, his hair greying – recalling the occasion when he and his comrades on board their troopship saw me standing on the quay and heard the melancholy notes of 'Will Ye No Come Back Again' floating over the ever-widening stretch of water between ship and quay.

He sounded almost apologetic as he went on. 'I want to say thank you for what your voice did for our morale.' Then, he added, softly, 'You will not take exception if I tell you that to me and my friends it was because you looked, and you were, so motherly that you were able to grip our emotions and give us the courage to carry on. You were then, and you will remain for us, the mother of all men.'

I was in Perth to attend a reunion – the greatest ever held in peacetime – of the 51st Highland Division. There is nothing so nostalgic or so salutary as a regimental reunion – particularly when the gaps of the years run into decades, and as I gazed over the soft green turf, with the music of the pipes in the background, I felt that my life had, at this moment, come full circle.

Here I was, being reminded of that electrifying moment in my life when I was called 'Ma', and here I was among the men who had been alongside my son Roy when he was killed fighting in Italy. There could be no two greater emotional flashbacks to those years that were compounded of so much tragedy, so much sorrow and suffering and so much heroism and inspiring self-sacrifice.

There were more than 10,000 members of the 51st Highland Division gathered in Perth – men bearing the proud distinction of having served with the Gordons, with the Black Watch, the Camerons, the Seaforths and the Argylls – and for me, specially invited to this great occasion, there were two functions I had to fulfil. One was to take advantage of this first opportunity I had had in twenty years to talk about my son Roy with the men who had been with him in the battle that was to be his last, and the other was to recall the dockside days when I had sung to the men of the 51st Highland Division as they passed through Durban on the way to the fronts where, inevitably, they added further lustre to their regimental records.

It was a brilliant sunny day when I arrived at the scene of this historic celebration, to be met by an officer who escorted me first to the General Officer Commanding the Division, Major-General Derek Lang, DSO, OC, of the Camerons, who welcomed me as the Division's guest of honour. With him were the ten generals of the Division, to each of whom I was introduced, thrilling to the sight of their chests ablaze with medal ribbons. I met many other wonderful personalities that day, among them, the Rev. Dr.

Caskie who was known as the 'Tartan Pimpernel' for the part he played in helping prisoners – one of them was Major-General Lang – to escape from St. Valerys.

Highlight to the preliminaries to the main celebration was the arrival of the Lord Provost, Dr. Ritchie, who, in tune with the times we are living in, arrived by helicopter and presented an interesting contrast between the old and the new as he stepped from the machine wearing the ancient scarlet robes and regalia of his office. I was introduced to Dr. Ritchie in the GOC's tent, which I was told to regard as my base for the day's operations. From there I made many sorties, the first of which – by special request – to the Press tent. I was interviewed by the BBC for their overseas service and then answered scores of questions flung at me by the newspapermen who pressed me to recall wartime incidents that involved the Scots. The next day, and indeed throughout all my stay in Scotland, the newspapers carried photographs and stories about me and the fact that I had been invited by General Lang to be the guest of honour at this historic reunion.

From the Press tent I was taken by Gordon Phillips to his regimental marquee – that of the Black Watch – and in a moment I was surrounded by the men who had been Roy's comrades, the 'dyed in the wool' Jocks as he had described them in his letter. I spent more than an hour with them, in which time memories came flooding back for them and for me as they described their experiences, moments of happiness and sadness, shared with Roy, and as I listened, controlling my emotions with difficulty, I felt a sense of thankfulness that it was men such as these who had been with Roy up to the time of his death.

My self-discipline failed to withstand the onslaught of meeting David Urquhart, Roy's platoon sergeant, who was devoted to Roy and who, unaware that Roy's wounds on that night patrol had proved fatal, wrote a letter to him wishing him a speedy recovery. The letter reached me with the personal belongings that were returned to me and I treasure it deeply. As David Urquhart spoke of Roy the phrases that flowed from him, in rich Scots accents, painted for me so vivid a picture of the love and admiration that his men had for him that I was no longer able to restrain the tears and I reached out and helped myself to the initialled pocket handkerchief that peeped from David Urquhart's breast pocket. At the sight of my distress sympathetic arms closed around my shoulders and words of comfort soon dispelled the momentary sadness that had enveloped us. I regained my composure before resuming my round of visits, and then watched the celebrations that culminated in the magnificent spectacle of the march past of the massed pipe and drum bands of the Highland regiments, the brilliant tartans and red hackles making a wonderful splash of colour against the background of the green sward. Even the sun co-operated that day to give added lustre to the scene; and as it began dipping below the horizon its rays flashed and glinted off the tunic buttons of the marching men.

I was given 20 minutes in which to dine and to dress in readiness for the function in the Perth City Hall where, on arrival, I was given a standing ovation. Wearing once more my white dress and red hat we recaptured in song, that evening, the wartime dockside days with the emphasis, not unnaturally, on those wonderful Scottish airs with which I used to greet ships with Scots aboard. It was a great and memorable evening summed up the following day by the Scottish *Sunday Express* which had a banner headline across its front page:

'15,000 men attend the greatest-ever peacetime re-union of soldiers – and Perla is their darling'.
'The Lady in Tartan brings back an army of memories.'

These Scottish days were crammed with activity and it seemed that not an hour went by without some incident, reunion, or meeting with friends, bringing back a flood of wartime memories.

How well I recalled that cold, rainy day in October 1943 when, in response to a shouted request 'Sing us a Scottish song' I sang 'Bonnie Mary of Argyll', and from the wild burst of cheering I knew that the Argylls were among the Scottish regiments on board the troopship. It was a big convoy that came in that day, the ships including the *Britannic*, the *Highland Chieftain*, the *Majola*, *Vollendam*, *Tamaroa*, *Larges Bay*, *Moreton Bay*, and *Esperance Bay*. Among the men in the ships was one who later gave an account of his ship's arrival in Durban to a Glasgow newspaper in which he said that he often wondered about an unknown soprano at an overseas port who brought tears to the eyes of hundreds of Scottish soldiers and a lump in the throats of many more.

With my son Roy serving with the Black Watch and my other son, Barrie, in the 1st Transvaal Scottish, a regiment affiliated to the Black Watch, I naturally had a close personal affinity with the Scots, and in the post-war years I never missed an opportunity of visiting Scotland to renew friendships that I had made in the war years. And Scotland responded with equal warmth. A famous Scottish newspaper, the *People's Journal* of Dundee, even went to the lengths in February 1946 of telephoning me at my home in Durban – the first overseas call I had ever received – to thank me for the 'wonderful work you have done for our lads in the war'. The voice, with a rich Scots accent, belonged to Mr. G.G. Glass, who later sent me a copy of the newspaper in which an account of our telephone conversation appeared. The article said that in response to many requests from servicemen and women who still spoke of the Lady-in-White the newspaper decided to telephone to convey a message of thanks and to tell the Lady-in-White of the conquest she had made of Scottish hearts. The article added: 'I distinctly noted the smile in her voice when she replied "Bless them all. I'll never forget them."'

Many questions were asked in that interview – it lasted 13 minutes and cost £13 and disposed of the notion that the Scots are tight-fisted – and I answered them all, describing how I came first to sing at the docks, telling them of my own family's connexion with Scotland; of the deep affection I and all other South Africans held for the Scots, and then giving this final message; 'I should like to send my love to you all and when I say that I speak for the whole of South Africa. We loved having them with us and we loathed seeing them go.'

On other post-war visits I met Colonel Kennedy, whose son, Ronald, had stayed with us in Pineholme before sailing in the *Laconia* to meet his death in the Mediterranean; Colonel Brian Madden, OC of the regiment Roy had served in; the regimental padre, the Rev. J. Grant, and many editors of newspapers, including Mr. Glass, who had telephoned me from Dundee. I was received by the Lord and Lady Provost of Dundee and with them sang many old Scottish songs to a gathering of elderly people whom they visited on Christmas Day. I have an album of photographs of that occasion, which was given an added significance for me by my being kissed by a white-haired old padre who told me that throughout the war he had worked among seamen in the dock area and that they had never tired of recounting to him their gratitude for what they termed the 'morale boost' they received from my singing in Durban.

These and other memories overwhelmed me when, as I said, I stood in 1963 with the men of the 51st Highland Division and shared with them recollections of their regimental glories. My thoughts kept returning to the words of that highlander, 'To us you were the mother of all men', and again I tried, as I have so often done in the past, to analyse my feelings as I stood on the dockside and sang. 'You must have had a tremendous sense of satisfaction', is a phrase that has been frequently used by people asking me for my reactions. The answer to that is no. I had a completely detached feeling – that what I was doing emanated not from me but through me. I was doing something as instinctively and as naturally as a mother would do for her child. It was a destiny I was born to fulfil. It seemed as if that highlander was right; that I, at a certain moment in history, became in my small way 'the mother of all men'. Has any grander title ever been bestowed on a woman? I doubt it.

But if singing has provided me with life's greatest fulfilment painting has been a close companion, especially when in 1958 the death occurred of my husband Jack, and left a void which I tried to fill by throwing myself with fervour into my painting. I am never more engrossed than when painting portraits, which call for total perfection of draughtsmanship and understanding of the sitter's personality. Some of the best achievements have been of Zulu people who, especially in their tribal surroundings, are perfect models.

The zenith of my painting career was attained a few years before the outbreak of World War II when I learned that the Royal Academy had accepted my 'White Roses', an oil painting, and that other pictures of mine were being hung in the Paris Salon, the Royal Scottish Academy, the Royal Hibernian Academy, the Royal Cambrian Academy and the Southport Modern Exhibition. Many exhibitions of my paintings have also been held in South Africa.

It seems almost appropriate, somehow, that one of my paintings – a six-foot square panel of the Umtata Falls, should have gone to the bottom of the sea – sunk by enemy action. It happened in 1942 when the SS *Umtata*, with full cargo and 38 passengers on board, was hit by torpedoes from a submarine which had crept into the harbour of Castries in which the *Umtata* was berthed. The painting I had done of the Umtata Falls consituted the main feature of the décor of the ship's lounge and it was undamaged when the *Umtata* settled on the shallow bottom of the harbour. Refloated, in due course, and with a large concrete slab in the hole where the torpedo had hit her, the ship set sail for the United States to undergo more permanent repairs. But her luck ran out when she was 10 miles off Miami. She was torpedoed again and this time there was no shallow bottom for her to settle on. She went straight down – 300 fathoms. The crew was saved, but my painting, with the rest of the ship, found a watery grave.

For me my most prized painting is one in which I have succeeded in capturing on a single canvas the likenesses of those who are most dear to me. I began by painting a life-sized portrait of my husband Jack, with an air force background, but found there was room to add other portraits. When my son Barrie came back from leave his likeness took its place alongside that of Jack; then I added my daughter Joy and finally, using a tiny photograph of Roy taken just before he left Cairo for Italy, I added his posthumous portrait to the group.

In my home in Durban – the 'high seat' as Douglas Reed called it – I am surrounded with countless mementoes of a life that has known every cadence. My memories, spanning very nearly three quarters of a century, are of a richness that comes only from having personally been a participant in virtually every human activity that makes up the sum total of life as we know it.

My faith . . . ? I am a great believer in prayer. I prayed for courage and I know that as a result of those prayers I was able to go out to the dockside, again and again throughout all the war years, laden as many of them were with tragedy, sadness and despair, and to sing as I have never sung before.

In the course of the war I received scores of verses and songs from well-wishers scattered around the world. Frequently there was thrown to me from the deck of a berthing troopship a piece of doggerel, or a regimental song to be sung to some popular melody. Some were typed, some hastily scribbled on the first scrap of paper that came to hand. I have kept them all. To me they are constant and sentimental reminders of the innermost thoughts of men reconciling themselves to adversity or conveying expressions of love and gentleness that normally would have no place in a soldier's vocabulary.

The most recent verse I have received was in commemoration of my 74th birthday and was written by my nearest neighbours, Professor Orlando and Edna Oldham. It says in a few brief words what I hope and believe are sentiments shared by the many, many men and women to whom an unknown voice, raised in song, helped to lift from their hearts, if only for a moment, the heavy burdens they were called upon to bear.

> An emblem of goodwill we see in you,
> A quality of mind clear to view
> Of those who've known you e'en a little while,
> 'Tis truth endorsed by every rank and file.
> And we who've known you now for many years,
> Oft think of you with feeling that bestirs.
> In thought, in word, in action, you have shown
> Some qualities of mind not many own.
> On us indeed, you've showered a wealth of love,

Inspired, you must have been, by Him above.
On others you have placed this wondrous gift,
It's fragrance sweet, does many souls uplift.
If e'er the history of your days is writ,
It will, with other things, disclose your wit,
Your passion in your aim to brighten life,
To see the good in all, to banish strife.
And it will show that in the World War time,
You played a role that truly was sublime.
With your melodious voice, you warriors pleased,
With food and other gifts, you eased their needs.
Enough! And now we wish our dear old friend,
A birthday in which joy and health transcend.
We further pray that many birthdays more
And happy ones, for her be still in store.

Epilogue

I returned home to Durban in December 1963 after my memorable visit to England and Scotland to find that any thoughts I may have had that my dockside singing career had finally come to its end were far from reality.

Without waiting to unpack cases, I went hurrying down to the docks in response to a message received that an old friend, HMS *Jaguar*, was in harbour. Not having been able to welcome her as she sailed through the harbour entrance I went down to Maydon Wharf where she was berthed to make amends and received a great welcome from the 'old hands' on board. Petty Officer John Thompson, who had served in HMS *Renown* in war-time, was particularly glad to see me and later he confided his special reasons for being so. He had told the 'young hands' that the Lady-in-White was certain to be there to welcome the ship and had begun to believe that their scepticism had some basis in fact when, as the ship sailed over the bar, there was no familiar Lady-in-White at her usual place on the North Pier. But he did not give up hope and his relief in seeing me at Maydon Wharf was expressed in his delighted cheering with the rest of the crew – He shouted: 'There she is – I told you so!'

Also at this time I welcomed South Africa's newest ship, SAS *President Kruger*, which, with an escort of four other vessels, sailed into Durban under command of Lieut.-Commander Terry Lloyd, to whom I had often sung before. I was there in my 'regulation uniform' and megaphone and as I sang, in acknowledgement to the salute that was accorded me, I felt then as I feel now that every memory that

this book may succeed in stirring in the hearts of those who
read it owes its origin to those simple but moving words:

> 'I sang a song into the air
> And the song, from beginning to end,
> I found again
> In the heart of a friend.'

Postscript

by Joy Liddiard

My late husband, Major Howard Liddiard, came through Durban in the convoy days of 1942. When his troopship docked he was first down the gangway to thank my Mom, 'The Lady in White', for her welcome and she responded with an open invitation for Howard and his friends to come to dinner at Pineholme. In those days of unbearably cramped conditions on troopships we soon learned that the most valued hospitality we could offer was often a hot bath and a meal in the atmosphere of home and family.

In 1949 my cousin, Peggy Gibson, and I treated ourselves to a trip to this England we'd heard so much about during the war and, when our funds ran low, found temporary secretarial work in the Westminster area.

Howard Liddiard learned of this and came to call. Two years later we were married at Holy Trinity, Brompton, on 5th April, 1952. My father was already committed to give cousin Peggy away ten days later in Durban but Mom flew over to give me away and had made my wedding dress; she had also gathered my bouquet of pink Anthuriums from the garden in Durban. The reception was at Victoria League, after which she left us in order to visit my brother Roy's grave in Italy; as told in her own story. I settled down to make England my permanent home.

Through the years I have had several lovely holidays in South Africa, while Mom made many trips to Britain to see the family and to renew old acquaintances. Amongst these were Ronald Kennedy's parents in St. Andrews, Fife – we'd known Ronald on HMS *Barham*; Major Simon Crawford in

Lochearnhead, Perthshire, who also managed to attend my wedding, as did another great friend, John Whitehouse, who we got to know well in the days when HMS *Illustrious* visited Durban; members of HMS *Dorsetshire* and *Cumberland* survivors at their reunion in 1970; the Burma Star Reunion in the Royal Albert Hall in 1964; the Star & Garter Home for disabled sailors and soldiers in 1955, and also St. Dunstans; Chelsea Barracks to sing in their chapel; and so many other old friends. Plus several pilgrimages with the War Graves Commission. Mom lived such an incredibly full life that it would take many chapters simply to record my memories of meeting those who knew and loved her, so I trust those left out or forgotten will not be hurt.

In 1953 my son, Andrew, was born and 5 years later, my daughter, Sally-Ann. I took Andrew home to meet my family when he was 15 months old and, in 1958 when my daughter was born, my parents planned a holiday in England; but this was not to be as Dad was found to be suffering terminal cancer. As he and Howard had never met, we all flew out as soon as it was deemed safe to travel with Sally-Ann, whereby my father met my husband and his new granddaughter only a few weeks before he died, on the 6th April 1958. We stayed with Mom for some time afterwards, although Howard had to leave us there in order to return to work. Once reunited we moved up to the Manchester area where Howard was with Shell-Mex & BP Limited as a construction engineer. We lived in Flixton.

My husband sadly died in 1976 and with the children both married and settled in the south – Andrew, a Lieutenant Commander in the Royal Navy, with his wife Carolyn and family, based at Portsmouth and Sally-Ann in Sherborne where her husband Phillip Stallwood teaches music – I finally moved from Flixton to live near my daughter in Sherborne. I have four grandchildren,

Wedding of Joy and Howard Liddiard at the Holy Trinity Church, Brompton, London, on 5th April 1952 – Joy's mother 'The Lady in White' gave her away!

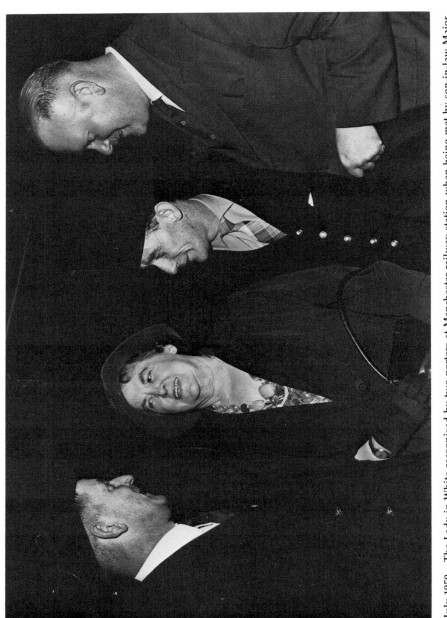

July 1959 – The Lady-in-White recognised by two porters at Manchester railway station when being met by son-in-law Major Howard Liddiard during a visit to the family.

Andrew's two boys, Simon and Christopher and Sally-Ann's son James and daughter Emma.

I have lived in Britain for 37 years now and although most of my relations, including my brother Barrie and his family, still live in Durban, the pain of separation has gradually lessened since my Mom died in 1971. I think I can safely say I am here to stay, and its certainly a good place to be.

Through the years and wherever we go, we meet people who remember The Lady in White – near Grimsby, where we lived while Howard handled a project there for his company and when my mother came over in 1954 to the 'Ask Pickles' programme, a dustman recognised her at the breakfast table as he passed our kitchen window; in London at the time of my wedding, a taxi driver did a U-turn in the busy road outside the Church when he recognised her; in Manchester, a railway porter recognised her when he carried her luggage; the vicar of Sherborne Abbey knew her (he has recently retired); several of our neighbours remember her well and so many others either knew her or know of her from war-time stories. Letters are still being written to the press asking news of her and to this very day, republishing the autobiography of The Lady in White is as a result of such enquiries.

Today, there are three memorials to the memory of The Lady in White in Durban. First, is the stone cairn which the Royal Navy asked the Durban City Council to erect on the North Pier where she used to sing. Its bronze plaque was cast in the workshop of the aircraft carrier, HMS *Eagle*, and a special unveiling and dedication ceremony was conducted with full naval ceremony by the *Eagle* ship's company. Second, the Perla Siedle Gibson Library, a mobile library run by the British Sailors' Society in Durban, for British seamen on all ships. And third, a five room unit at the Highway Hospice for which funds were raised in memory of The

Lady in White, at a ball in the City Hall and an exhibition of her paintings in 1985.

> "She is naive and childlike in her uncritical faith in the good in life . . . . She still trusts life: she trusts people: the divinity which protects babes and drunks takes a little time off to protect Perla too."

These words written by Noel Langley in a Candid Cameo published in *The Sketch* are very true – Mom had a strong faith and believed in the power of prayer. Several of our Christian friends prayed for her protection in those dark dangerous days and nights, when she'd stand for hours in all weathers, quite alone on the dockside, lifting the hearts of the men on troopships, with some of their favourite songs from home. At times of great need for strength to carry on, as for instance when I received the news of my brother Roy's tragic death and had to interrupt a singing lesson at Mom's studio. Before going home we called on one of these wonderful supportive friends who immediately undertook to pray us through the darkness that enveloped us.

Again, when her eye was shattered as described later, Mom's first reaction was to cover her face with her hands, drop to her knees and pray for help.

The fact is that her whole life and the wonderful way she soldiered through the ups and downs of life are a perfect witness to her faith which in itself was a gift from God. She always believed He had a plan for her life and ours, and He would carry us through if we were obedient to His calling. Our days if humanly possible, always started with Bible reading and prayer, a habit that is well proven, and for which I personally give thanks. It is nothing short of a miracle that after the rigours of singing out of doors in all weathers for so many hours day after day and at night as well, a throat specialist was amazed to find her throat and in particular her vocal chords were totally unimpaired.

As is promised, "We know that in everything God works for good with those who love Him, who are called according to His purpose." (Rom. 8:28).

Among the trunkloads of memorabilia she left was a tape made at a reunion of HMS *Dorsetshire* and HMS *Cumberland* survivors held at Durban, August 1969. Here's what she said when introduced at what was possibly her last public appearance:

> 'I sang a song into the air
> And the song from beginning to end
> I found again in the heart of a friend.'

This is August 1969 and I, Perla Siedle Gibson, have been asked by veterans of the Allied Forces – to whom I was privileged to sing a welcome from the North Pier of Durban Harbour during two World Wars – to record my story for them.

I was trained as a concert painist and singer in Durban, London, New York, Paris and Berlin.

During the Kaiser War, when the volunteers from Australia, New Zealand, and South Africa passed through Durban, my mother and her friends ran a Services canteen in which I was frequently called upon to sing, as well as on the dockside.

It was during that time that my eldest brother was killed at the Somme offensive.

In the Hitler war, history repeated itself when again my parents organised refreshments for the first contingent of Rhodesians to go en route through Durban to the East African battlefields early in 1940. As their ships sailed, the lads called for me to sing.

My husband, Jack Gibson, BEM served with No 2 Fighter Squadron of the South African Air Force; our two sons, Roy and Barrie, with the 1st Transvaal Scottish; and our daughter, Joy, drove for the South African Women's Auxiliary Service.

Roy, our elder son, was seconded to the 6th Battalion, the Black Watch Royal Highland Regiment as Lieutenant C.R. Gibson, and was killed in action in Italy.

My war work took rather a different turn when, once again, I was up to my elbows in dockside canteen work, wearing a white dress and apron – as a result of which I became known as 'The Lady in White'.

When called upon to sing to the convoys entering and leaving Durban, the Defence Force gave me the freedom of the docks and a permit marked 'Dockside Entertainment'. Although an experienced operatic soprano of long standing, my voice had by now developed to withstand all weathers and at all hours – outdoors, or course – in response to the call from the ships to, 'Give us a song, Ma!'.

To be in time to welcome convoys as they were piloted, ship by ship, into the safety of Durban harbour, entailed motoring down at dawn through the town and through the sprawling dockyard area to the farthermost point – North Pier. There I'd sing 'Rule Britannia' to warships and 'Land of Hope and Glory' to the troopships. Then back to the wharfs to respond to requests at the ships' sides amounting at times to more than 200 songs in a day.

During the postwar visits made to South Africa by the Royal Family I was honoured to be nominated for first presentation on two separate occasions. Their Majesties said they had heard much of what I had done for the morale of their fighting forces and, as so many have done, asked how it all came about.

At the end of the war, official sources calculated that I'd been given the privilege of singing Godspeed to over three million Service-men and -women aboard warships, hospital-ships, refugee-ships and several other classes of sea-going vessels.

Now, at the age of 81, I continue to be at my post to greet the Royal Navy as often as I can.

That gives you the story as briefly as I can, and now . . . Thanks for the memories – and some songs!'

A dramatic feature of the foregoing is that she made that appearance with one good eye and a matching glass one. A year earlier and, while they were jointly trimming the overhang of a large avocado tree, her gardener swung wildly at an offending frond with their panga-like pruning knife and shattered Mom's right eye with the handle-end. The 'Natal Mercury' of 22 February 1968 reported as follows:

In a room full of flowers the cheerful 79-year-old sat up in bed at the hospital last night and told of how she sunk to her knees and prayed when it happened. 'The pain was unbelievable', she said.

But now she's feeling fine after doctors operated to remove the eye. She displayed the first couplet of a poem she'd started:
'My love for the Navy I hoped I'd proved well enough
But to emulate Nelson and lose an eye is altogether too tough!'

Once she'd been fitted with a glass eye my Mom quickly adjusted to her handicap. My cousin, Barbara Siedle, wrote to Sam Morley last year when he was searching for more background information with which to complete this book. She was very close to Mom, with common interests in music and painting. She wrote:

I remember Perla with her glass eye after the accident 21 years ago. I particularly remember how it affected her painting once she could take it up again. She said she had to put out her left hand to touch the place on the canvas where she wanted to apply paint. She still continued to paint vigorously and flamboyantly as was her characteristic style.

I went on quite a few painting outings with her when she came to stay with us in the Cape. My Mom would drop us off at Hout Bay Harbour, for example, and even with the wind and sand blowing she would complete a vibrant, colourful rendition of the boats and mountains while I could only manage a few miserable brush strokes and pencil lines on my canvas. I'd love to have her around to talk art with now.

I once painted Perla with the suggestion of her singing to a warship in the background – having been commissioned by the Highway Cancer Hospice in Durban who named their new wing after her.

"We may forget many things of this war," said an American writer in 1944, "but never the songs of Durban's Lady in White." To that, and in Durban, The Lady in White commented, "In a year or two I'll have been forgotten. Men have more important things to remember than a little old lady who sang to them as they sailed away to war."

(From *Durban Daily News*, 22nd February, 1968)

Now I feel like Nelson she says

There's no defeating the "Lady in White"—Mrs. Perla Siedle Gibson, who became famous for greeting naval ships at Durban in the war with a song. A knife slipped and she has lost her right eye. But she is still smiling, still capable of joking about her mishap. "Now I feel like Nelson," she says.

In remembrance of Perla

Daily News Reporter

A STONE cairn, soon to bear a bronze plaque commemorating Durban's war-time morale boosting "Lady in White, Mrs Perla Siedle Gibson, has been completed at the end of North Pier near where she used to stand to welcome and farewell ships.

The plaque is being made in the Royal Navy Admiralty dockyards in England. It will be presented to Durban by the senior Royal Navy officer in South Africa, Commodore A. Cecil, possibly when he visits the city at the end of the month.

It will symbolise the navy's thanks on behalf of the 3-million troops who visited Durban on their way to and from the fronts during World War 2 and heard the voice of the Lady in White echoing across the water.

Throughout the war, come rain or shine, at dawn or sunset, if there was a ship arriving or leaving, the white-clad woman with red hat and megaphone stood at the harbour entrance to sing her serenade.

It has been estimated that she sang 250 songs a day for six years, and won the hearts of thousands all over the world.

A legend in her own lifetime, Mrs Gibson died last year at the age of 82

● Picture: The monument on North Pier. A ship sailing from Durban provides an appropriate background: Inset: The "Lady in White" as she will be remembered by thousands.

TO THE MEMORY OF PERLA GIBSON
"THE LADY IN WHITE"
WHO SANG TO COUNTLESS THOUSANDS OF
BRITISH COMMONWEALTH AND ALLIED SERVICEMEN
AS THEY PASSED THROUGH DURBAN OVER THE YEARS
1940 TO 1971
THIS TABLET WAS PRESENTED BY THE
OFFICERS AND MEN OF THE ROYAL NAVY

But just look at what's transpired since then.

When she celebrated her eightieth birthday in 1969 she was showered with cards, telegrams and gifts from the remotest corners of the world. They arrived from the Far West of America, from the open spaces of Australia, from the mountains of Norway and the bulb fields of Holland.

Two years later she died peacefully at her home in Durban. The occasion was marked by almost every newspaper in the world running double-page spreads on this fabulous lady and her wartime career.

And now, 47 years after that American writer's forecast and in answer to current demand, comes this 27-year-old autobiography.

I'd say the prophetic American writing man knew what he was talking about and that my Mom had it wrong – wouldn't you!

Joy Liddiard

Christmas, 1990

On page 188 Barbara Siedle, Perla's niece, tells of a painting she did from photographs for the Highway Hospice in Durban. She kindly supplied a transparency when asked and explains the theme as follows:

'In an attempt to capture not only a portrait of Auntie Perla, but also that essence of her life for which she was so famous, I decided to paint the foreground as she was in later life against a picture taken of her in the war when singing to a troopship in Durban harbour.

She was frequently invited to parties aboard visiting ships and would sing to them as they left during the post-war years, whereby I saw her on numerous occasions in this characteristic pose of singing, smiling, and waving as a ship docked or left harbour.

This impressionistic picture is intended to capture what was, for me, the spirit of Perla Siedle Gibson.'

Barbara Siedle
February 1991

Appendix

Some of the ships to which the Lady-in-White sang during World War II:

10 April 1940. *Takliwa*.

16 April 1940. *Karanja*.

18 June 1940. HMS *Dragon*, HMS *Kent*, HMS *Cornwall*, *Reina del Pacifico, Orion, Lancashire, Devonshire, Dilwara, Capetown Castle, Nestor, Melbourne Star*.

1 September 1940. *Llangibby Castle. Franconia*, HMS *Dragon*, HMS *Kanimbla*.

27 September 1940. *Llanstephan Castle, Llangibby Castle*, HMS *Ceres*.

8 October 1940. HMS *Kanimbla, Empress of Britain, Andes, Strathaird, Empress of Canada*.

22 October 1940. *Duchess of Bedford, Empress of Japan, Orion*.

23 October 1940. HMS *Royal Sovereign*.

15–17 November 1940. *Britannic, Llandaff Castle, Llanstephen Castle, Selandia, Westernland*.

3 December 1940. HMS *Cornwall, Scythia, Highland Monarch, Almanzora, Malanchi, Martland, Deluis*.

5 December 1940. HMAS *Shropshire, Georgic, Monarch of Bermuda, Duchess of York, City of Paris*.

8 December 1940. *Llandaff Castle, City of Baroda*.

12 December 1940. *Strathallan, Strathaird, Strathnaven, Reina del Pacifico, Empress of Canada, Viceroy of India, Andes, Oreades, Duchess of Atholl, Otranto*, HMS *Devonshire*, HMS *Hawkins*, HMS *Shropshire*.

25 January 1941. *Otranto, Tamoroa, City of Derby, City of Canterbury, City of London, Rangitiki, Benrinnes, Neuralia,*

191

Menelaus, Costa Rica, Elizabethville, Empire Ability, Delane, HMS *Ceres,* HMS *Shropshire.*

28 January 1941. *Nieuw Holland.*

29 January 1941. *Strathallan, Empress of Canada, Sontay, Brutus,* HMS *Enterprise,* HMS *Hermes.*

11 February 1941. *Pennland, Britannia, Highland Princess, Duchess of Richmond, Ormonde, Highland Chieftain, Cameronia, Orbito, Neahellas, Franconia, Samaria,* HMAS *Australia.*

24 March 1941. *Rangitata, Northumberland, Matawa, Rushive, Almanzora, Bergensfjord, Bellerophon, Thysville, City of Hankow, Salween, Scythia, City of Corinth, Yoma, City of Pittsburgh, Llanstephan Castle, Consuelo, Logician, Mahseer, Dalesman, Manchester City,* HMS *Phoebe,* HMS *Cornwall, Dilwara, City of Canterbury, City of London.*

3 April 1941. *Duchess of Bedford, Duchess of Richmond, Samaria, Athlone Castle, Monarch of Bermuda, Franconia.*

19 April 1941. *Viceroy of India, Stirling Castle, Otranto, Glenorchy, Strathnaver, Warwick Castle, Denbighshire, Orontes, Mentor, Observer, Gunda, Johan van Oldenbarnefeldt.*

20 April 1941. *Dempo.*

22 April 1941. HMS *Nelson,* HMS *Napier, Nizam.*

10 May 1941. HMS *Eagle.*

16 May 1941. *Scythia, Bergensfjord, Leopoldville, Nova Scotia.*

21 May 1941. *Dilwara, City of Paris.*

27 May 1941. *Benghalis, Strathaird, Aronde, Empress of Russia, Sabriska, Dominion Monarch, Abbekerk, City of Exeter, Reina del Pacifico, Dalhana,* HMS *Hawkins.*

14 June 1941. *Duchess of York, Viceroy of India.*

15 June 1941. *City of Canterbury, Strathmore.*

16 June 1941. *Duchess of Athol, Orontes.*

20 June 1941. *Duchess of Richmond, Orduna, Martland, Almanzora, Georgic,* HMS *Barham,* HMS *Exeter.*

4 July 1941. *Orbita, Mooltan, Bergensfjord, Franconia, Samaria, Highland Brigade, Christiaan Huygens, British Merchant, Empire Condor, Empire Egret, Empire Curlew, Aagtekerk.*

5 July 1941. *Mauretania, Ile de France.*

7 July 1941. *Nieuw Amsterdam.*

15 July 1941. *Llandaff Castle, Nova Scotia, Dilwara.*

30 July 1941. *City of Exeter, Athlone Castle, Monarch of Bermuda, Oronsay, Tamaroa, Mataroa, Clan McFayden, Alamanzora,* HMS *Galatea.*

19 August 1941. *Duchess of Bedford, Orduna,* HMS *Primula.*

7 September 1941. *Tairea.*

9 September 1941. *Ile de France, Britannic, Monarch of Bermuda.*

10 September 1941. *City of Canterbury, Elizabethville, Indrapoera.*

11 September 1941. *Thysville, Nieuw Holland, Llandaff Castle.*

15 September 1941. *Arundel Castle.*

25 September 1941. *Amra.*

26 September 1941. *Llandovery Castle.*

28 September 1941. *Selandia,* HMS *Revenge.*

1 October 1941. *Mauretania, Nieuw Amsterdam,* HMAS *Australia.*

3 October 1941. *Mooltan, Sythia, Otranto, Manchester Progress, Empress of Australia, Barrister,* HMS *Repulse,* HMS *Encounter.*

18 October 1941. *Nieuw Amsterdam.*

22 October 1941. *Atlantis.*

27 October 1941. *Lancaster Vilendam, Durnera, Indrapoera.*

30 October 1941. *Rod el Farag, Neahellas, Strathaver.*

3 November 1941. HMS *Derbyshire,* HMS *Repulse, Samaria, Ormonde, Empress of Russia, Highland Brigade, Franconia, Alamanzora, Duchess of Richmond, Clan Lamont, Perseus, City of Paris.*

12 November 1941. *Eastern Prince.*

15 November 1941. *City of Canterbury*.

16 November 1941. *Nieuw Holland*.

17 November 1941. *Pulaski*.

18 November 1941. *Llandaff Castle, Kozcuissko, Elizabethville*, HMS *Emerald*, HMS *Colombo*.

20 November 1941. *Amra*.

1 December 1941. *Stratheden*.

2 December 1941. *Aronda*.

7 December 1941. *Nieuw Amsterdam, Mauretania*.

11 December 1941. *Aba*.

13 December 1941. *Empire Pride*.

17 December 1941. *Mataroa, Arundel Castle, Monarch of Bermuda, Aorangi, Capetown Castle, Empress of Asia, Abbekerk, Adrustus, Deucalion, Duchess of Bedford, Narkunda, Orduna, Empress of Japan, Rimutaka, Nieuw Amsterdam*, HMS *Royal Sovereign*, HMS *Milford*, HMS *Sussex*.

25 December 1941. *Alamanzora*.

26 December 1941. *Dundrum Castle*.

8 January 1942. *Duchess of Athol, Andes, Dunera, Highland Princess, Brajara, Athlone Castle, Oronsay, Durban Castle, Cameronia, Scythia, Reina del Pacifico, Strathallan*.

11 February 1942. *Atlantis*.

13 February 1942. *Otranto, Britannic, Arowa, Viceroy of India, Strathnaver, Stirling Castle, Worcestershire, Staffordshire, Christiaan Huygens, Empire Woodlark, Autolycus*.

3 March 1942. *Amra*.

21 March 1942. *Monarch of Bermuda, Duchess of York, Strathaird, Stratheden, Awatea, Duchess of Richmond, Ormonde, Vollendam, Empire Pride*.

26 March 1942. HMS *Newcastle*.

6 April 1942. *Otranto, Llandaff Castle*.

8 April 1942. HMS *Ceres*.

10 April 1942. *Atlantis, Orantes*.

11 April 1942. *Empire Success.*

15 April 1942. *Aba.*

16 April 1942. HMS *Valiant.*

21 April 1942. *Amra*, HMS *Ramillies.*

22 April 1942. *Oronsay, Duchess of Athol, Karanja, Keren, Sobieski, Mataroa, Largs Bay, Winchester Castle, Thalatta, Empire Kingsley, Franconia, Empress of Russia, Windsor Castle*, HMS *Malaya*. HMS *Illustrious.*

26 April 1942. HMS *Revenge.*

29 April 1942. *Felix Rousel.*

2 May 1942. *Vita.*

17 May 1942. *Atlantis, Capetown Castle, Empress of Japan, Nederland, Empire Peacock, Highland Princess, Highland Chieftain, Aorangi, Rangitala, Duchess of Bedford, Maloja, Clan Lamont, City of Capetown*, HMS *Carlisle, Foxhound*, HMS *Resolution.*

27 May 1942. *Dorsetshire.*

3 June 1942. *Tairea.*

9 June 1942. HMS *Ramillies*, HMS *Emerald, Pasteur, Ormonde, Strathaird, Moreton Bay, Orizaba, Maunganui.*

19 June 1942. HMS *Revenge, Foxhound, Anthony, Bragon, Franconia.*

30 June 1942. *Amra.*

2 July 1942. *Otranto, Andes, Christiaan Huygens, Viceroy of India, Orcades, Arawa, Warwick Castle, Britannic, Chateau Thiery, Christobel, Santa Paulo.*

20 July 1942. *Strathmore, Stirling Castle, Arundel Castle, Durban Castle, Empress of Russia, Awatea, Orion, Stratheden*, HMS *Wyvern, Brilliant, Swiftsure.*

27 July 1942. HMS *Hotspur*, HMS *Queen Elizabeth.*

8 August 1942. *Santa Rosa.*

11 August 1942. *Christiaan Huygens, Mauretania.*

19 August 1942. *Britannic, City of Windsor, Pulaski.*

3 September 1942. *Pulaski, Atlantis, Leopoldville*, HMS

Corsica, HMS *Duncan, Christiaan Huygens.*

17 September 1942. *Tairea.*

19 September 1942. *City of Canterbury, Windsor Castle, Nieuw Amsterdam.*

28 September 1942. *Highland Brigade, Highland Chieftain, Rangitata, Orcades, Sibijak, Boissevain, Mataroa,* HMS *Shropshire, Suffolk.*

21 October 1942. *J. van Rensselaar.*

24 October 1942. *Empire Trooper, Dilwara, Sontay, Dunera, Empire Woodlark, Vita.*

28 October 1942. HMS *Napier, Inconstant, Blackmore.*

30 October 1942. *Mauretania.*

31 October 1942. *Nieuw Amsterdam.*

2 November 1942. *Dorsetshire,* HMS *Erebus.*

5 November 1942. *Tairea, Capetown Castle, Highland Monarch, Empress of Russia, Morcambe Bay, Rimutaka, Straat Malakha, Silver Sandal, Port Jackson.*

17 November 1942. *Almanzora, California.*

18 November 1942. *Atlantis.*

19 November 1942. *Sontay.*

20 November 1942. *Selandia,* HMS *Resolution,* HMS *Jasmine, Nigella, Ganistra, Nepal, Napier, Fortune, Hotspur.*

3 December 1942. HMS *Inconstant.*

4 December 1942. *Empress of Scotland, Athlone Castle, Largs Bay, Stirling Castle, Arawa, Queen of Bermuda.*

31 December 1942. *Highland Monarch, Empire Trooper* HMS *Frobisher, Gambia, Nizem, Foxbound, Fritillery, Inconstant.*

18 January 1943. *Britannic, Orion, Rangitiki, Highland Princess, Esperance Bay, Mataroa, City of Lincoln, Manchester Division, British Chemist,* HMS *Cheshire, Express, Ceres, Quilliam.*

19 January 1943. *Dilwara, Streefkerk, Ingleton, Empire Southey, Norse Trader, Taygetos.*

23 January 1943. *Ascanius, Oronda, Felix Roussel,* HMS

Carthage, Birmingham, Blackmore, Prudent, Fortune.

11 February 1943. *Berwickshire, Fort Comousin, Atlantis, Ocean Strength, Herma Gorthon,* HMS *Dauntless.*

19 February 1943. *Vancouver City, Lancashire,* HMS *Arctic Explorer, Indian Star, Catterick.*

25 February 1943. *Maloja, Vollendam, Empress of Canada, Mooltan, Dominion Monarch, Stratheden, Dempo, Empire Trooper,* HMS *Ceres, Cilicia, Racehorse, Quickmarch, Quiberon.*

27 February 1943. *City of Canterbury, Elizabethville,* HMS *Norman, Albatross.*

8 March 1943. *Pulaski.*

20 March 1943. *Dilwara, Khedive, Ismail, Luxmi, Coulborm,* HMS *Chitral, Racehorse, Wayland, Devonshire, Relentless, Quality, Napier.*

26 March 1943. *Panaghiotis, Strathmore, Strathaird, Christiaan Huygens, Capetown Castle, Antenor,* HMS *Sussex, Foxhound, Quilliam, Freesia.*

29 March 1943. *Peleus, Griqua, Alamanzora,* HMS *Quail, Raider, Queensborough.*

2 April 1943. *Ile de France, City of Bristol.*

6 April 1943. HMS *Freesia, Raider, Norwich City, Lady Elsa, Herefordshire, Lady Rosemary.*

7 April 1943. *Dominion Monarch, Panaman, Peter C. Gallagher, Inchanga, Umgeni.*

14 April 1943. *Reina del Pacifico, Sobieski, Strathnaver, Otranto, Orontes, Perthshire,* HMS *Bololo, Rapier, Keren, Foxhound, Nigella, Rotherham.*

12 May 1943. *Clan MacIlwraith, Port Royal Park, City of Windsor, Black Healh, Welsh Trader, Seringa, Empire Woodlark, British Power,* HMS *Lady Rosemary, Gambia, Northern Duke, Indian Star, Marguerite, Aster.*

21 May 1943. *Straat Malakka, Orion, Highland Monarch, Highland Brigade, Clan Lamont,* HMS *Norman Redoubt,*

Quadrant.

2 June 1943. HMS *Northern Dawn, Sphere, Vereeniging, Falmouth, Quadrant, Redoubt, Verbena, Kathiawar, Kumoan, Masterful.*

22 August 1943. *Moreton Bay, Esperance Bay, Largs Bay, Britannic, Nea Hellas, Rangitata, Highland Chieftain, Tamaroa, Maloja,* HMS *Relentless, Rapid, Quiberon, Norman.*

25 August 1943. *Strathmore, Jersey City, Mormac Dove, Mormac Moon, Essa Baytown.*

2 September 1943. *Hoegh Hood, Highland Monarch, City of Lincoln, East Gate, Highland Brigade, Jose Menendez, Nederland.*

10 September 1943. HMS *Ramillies.*

13 October 1943. *Boessevain, Indrapoera, Duchess of Richmond, John A. Johnson, Antenor, Ormonde, Johan de Witt,* HMS *Teviot, Bann, Trent, Plym.*

10 November 1943. *Fort Maisonnease, Highland Brigade, Sheafcrown,* HMS *Caradock, Arctic Explorer, Quadrant, Relentless.*

16 November 1943. *City of Paris, Cape Warwick,* HMS *Emerald, Verbena.*

19 November 1943. *Streefkerk, Atlantian, Jersey City, Stella Polaris, Cap St. Jacques.*

6 December 1943. *Leighton, Empire Trooper, Pulaski,* HMS *Chitral, Test.*

5 January 1944. *Gawler, Maryborough, Marriet B. Stowe, City of Sydney, Walker Taylor, Astrida.*

4 February 1944. HMS *Suffolk, Battler.*

10 February 1944. *Nieuw Amsterdam, Radbury, Rocky Mountain Park, Ocean Volunteer,* HMS *Rapid.*

27 February 1944. *Elias G. Kukukundis, Eskbank, Edward Livingstone, Louis Joliet, Lieut. St. Loubert Bie, Empire Envoy.*

28 February 1944. *Empress of Scotland, Halvdan, Empire Woodlark, Frank Springer.*

3 March 1944. *T.J. Jackson, Point Pleasant Park, British Unity,* HMS *Falmouth.*

22 March 1944. *Shoreham, Talma, Clan MacGillivray, Fort Albany.*

31 March 1944. HMS *Emerald, John A. Robeling, Silverlaurel Ittersum.*

3 April 1944. *Fort Rouille, Baronesa, Chinese Prince, Diamnatis.*

5 April 1944. *City of Newcastle, Honesty, Star of Egypt, Nikos.*

9 April 1944. *Vita, Delane, Empire Success, Ville d'Amiens, Patrick Henry, Nestor.*

13 April 1944. *Inventor, City of Dundee, Dahlia, Clan Forbes, Radcombe, Frontier,* HMS *Rocket, Pathfinder,* USSN *Wake Island, Mission Bay.*

30 April 1944. *Themistocles, Plym, Monarch of Bermuda.*

13 May 1944. *English Prince,* USSN *General Butner.*

15 May 1944. *Port Jackson, Radbury, City of Rangoon.*

30 May 1944. *Norton, Empire Chivalry, Joseph Francis, Sheafholme, Pallenberg, Calgary.*

4 July 1944. *Rhesus, Martand, Stensby, Pendit, Menelaus, Nasea, Starstone, Buffalo Park, Jose J. Acosta, Baltavia.*

13 July 1944. *Empire Chieftain, Fort Machault, Empire Nile, Unita, Radcombe, Industria, Suncrest.*

18 July 1944. *City of Bristol, Empire Lancer.*

22 July 1944. *Empire Prince, Olympos, Halvdan, Manchester Commerce, Ocean Viscount, Rajput, Kronviker, Spey Hunt.*

15 August 1944. HMS *Illustrious, Paladin, Roebuck.*

3 September 1944. *Salween, Empire Woodlark, Hong Kneng, Shirala,* HMS *Fingborn, Lulworth, Sennen.*

6 September 1944. *Ocean Vestal, Radfield, Selandia,* HMS *Ceylon.*

1 October 1944. *Geo W. Ather, Californian, Baron Cawser, Empire Captain, Joseph Goldberger.*

3 October 1944. *Pundit, Geologist, Frame, David Holmes,* HMS *Queen Elizabeth, Rotherham, Rapid.*

26 October 1944. *John A. Brown, City of Calcutta, Collegian.*

31 October 1944. *Nederland, City of Paris, Kosciuszko, Baron Fairlie,* HMS *Fishguard, Banff, Stella Polaris, Totland, Snowflake.*

27 November 1944. *Wairuna, Orari,* HMS *Thyme, Rebecca Boone.*

29 November 1944. *Samtrusty, Tower Hill, Ocean Valentine, City of Rangoon.*

1 December 1944. *Asutralind, Queen Adelaide.*

3 December 1944. *Nestor, Middlesex Trader.*

14 December 1944. *Straat Soenda.*

18 December 1944. HMS *Renown.*

1 February 1945. *Selandia, British Judge, Empire Malacca.*

2 March 1945. *Sarpedon, Alfios, Ingra Maersk, Rancher, Empire Kitchener, Pegu, Astrida,* HMS *Lossie.*

4 March 1945. *Sanderwent, Sarddring, Houston City, Empire Dynasty, Star of Alexandria.*

12 March 1945. *Glenartney, City of Canterbury, Elizabethville, Thysville, Clan Ranald,* HMS *Teal, Falmouth, Jasmine.*

16 April 1945. *Beaton Park, Samshire, Middlesex Trader, Princess Audrey.*

22 April 1945. *City of Sydney, Empire Addison,* HMS *Awe, Rockrose.*

31 May 1945. HMS *Burrcross, Monkshood.*

15 June 1945. *Fort Musquarro, Nieuw Amsterdam, Samoa, Ocean Viceroy, Richmond Castle, Rijoletto.*

25 June 1945. HMS *Venus, Virago.*

27 June 1945. HMS *Howe.*

2 July 1945. *City of Canterbury,* HMSAS *Spindrift,* HMSAS *Natal.*

15 August 1945. (VJ Day). *City of Calcutta, Dunkeld, Reina del Pacifico, Empire Might, Fort*

Editor's Note and Acknowledgments

Thanks to trunk-loads of 30-to-90-year-old memorabilia in Joy Liddiard's home, plus contributions from Barbara Siedle in Durban, there's been no shortage of press cuttings and photographs to supplement Perla's text. Some a bit yellowed and dog-eared, but the printer did a grand job when reproducing them.

With regard to the text, I've tried not to stray too far from Perla's subjective writing style when editing the original work but still finished up with a fair sprinkling of superfluous 'I's and 'me's. But that's 'par for the course', so to speak, coming as it does from a professional concert star who had enjoyed international centre-stage treatment throughout her colourful public life.

Debts of gratitude are due to:

Those newspapers and photographic agencies whose work has been used but who, due to passing years and distance, may not have been approached individually for prior permission.

Purnell & Sons Pty Ltd of South Africa, publishers of the *Lady in White* in 1964, who raised no objection to this English version.

Chronicle of the Union Castle Line, 1853 to 1953 by Mareschal Murray, for the photograph of *Capetown Castle* between decks and some of the statistics on page 86.

Reg and Joan Davies for their help in preparing the Index, and

Helen Wightwick for converting their hieroglyphical sheets of script into a legible typescript for the printer. Also for the part she played with Destiny in the origination of this work, as described in the Introduction. Not to mention her secretarial services throughout the preparation and marketing of it.

HMS *Dorsetshire* Association for the relevant photographs and copy of their 1971 magazine from which excerpts were taken for the captions to photograph facing page 110.

And so many more who have helped or shown encouraging interest in the publication of this book.

INDEX

(Ships named in the Appendix do not appear here unless also included in the text)